Alabama Gardens Great and Small

A GUIDED TOUR

By Ed Givhan and Jennifer Greer

with Peggy Givhan and Charlotte Hagood

Beech Hill Inc.

First Printing 2002
Printed at Ebsco Media, Birmingham, Ala., U.S.A.
Published by Beech Hill Inc.
P. O. Box 67
Safford, AL 36773

The Library of Congress has catalogued this book as follows:

Givhan, Ed
Alabama Gardens Great and Small: A Guided Tour /
Ed Givhan and Jennifer Greer, with Peggy Givhan and Charlotte Hagood. - 1st ed.

Library of Congress
Control Number
2001099371
ISBN 0-9701993-0-9

Other books by Ed Givhan include "Flowers for South Alabama"
and "Conversations with a Southern Gardener."

Other books by Jennifer Greer include "Alabama Gardener's Guide."

Visit www.alabamagardening.com

Acknowledgements

Special thanks to Robert Gandy, Lawrence Rives,
Jane Hagood, Gene and Bob Lightfoot,
Mark Moore, Cathy Vinzant, Patsy Wallace, Jane Henry,
Verna Gates, Kim Searcy, Harry Murphy,
Minuteman Press, David and Julie Bagwell, Helen Phillips,
Dr. Joe Sledge, Jennifer Fairley,
all of the gardeners who were interviewed
and everyone who supported the creation of this book.

Table of Contents

Preface

Preface

"The garden-lover, who longs to transfer something of the old garden-magic to his own patch of ground at home, will ask himself…. What can I bring away from here?…. Not this or that amputated statue, or broken bas-relief, or fragmentary effect of any sort, but a sense of the informing spirit – an understanding of the gardener's purpose, and the uses to which he meant his garden to be put."

Edith Wharton
"Italian Villas and Their Gardens"

Ed and Peggy Givhan stood in a garden near the village of Houdan in the Ile-de-France. Passionate gardeners, they had journeyed all the way from Montgomery, Ala., to see the gardens of Europe. As they looked at the formal French garden, with its exquisite parterres and flower borders, inspiration struck.

"We can do that," said Peggy, ever confident.

"I know," Ed responded, realizing they had been in France for only 24 hours – and he couldn't wait to get back home to his garden.

Today, the Givhans enjoy a superb French parterre garden in Montgomery. When out-of-town guests voice surprise at seeing such an elegant formal garden, Ed smiles, turns up his favorite Chopin sonata and offers them another glass of Bordeaux. (Never mind that he drives a pick-up truck and listens to country music on the weekends.) The Givhans also

enjoy a country cottage garden in Safford, in the heart of Alabama's Black Belt.

They are among many gardeners who have taken to traveling to learn about the great gardens of the world. This is not to encourage imitation, but to stimulate learning, inspiration and reinvention of the best.

In 1998, Ed called and asked me and Charlotte Hagood to collaborate with him and

Ed and Peggy Givhan's garden in at Furman House in Montgomery was inspired by a private estate, La Mormaire, in France. Formal parterres define the garden. Exuberant flower beds reflect English influences. A far pergola is borrowed from the Italian Renaissance tradition. The Givhans' garden is an elegant amalgam of styles.

Peggy on a book about Alabama gardens. We photographed more than 60 gardens, public and private, and met some of the most sharing people that we know. In the process, we discovered a new way to look at Alabama gardens. Charlotte calls it "learning to see."

Eddie Aldridge of Aldridge Gardens

First, we learned that many great Alabama gardens share strong stylistic links with the great gardens of the world. We can boast everything from Italian villas and French parterres to English cottage gardens and contemporary arboreta and ecological preserves in this state. If we have the inclination to travel abroad, we will no doubt enjoy and benefit from it. Yet there is much to be learned, appreciated and promoted about great gardens – in Alabama.

Second, we recognize that today's Alabama gardeners have inherited important public gardens from the last century. These gardens grew out of the efforts of garden patrons and community leaders with a broader vision of educa-

tion and the arts, with names like Bellingrath, Fitzpatrick, Inscoe, Blount, Warner, Ireland, Jemison, Kaul, Spencer and Aldridge, to name but a few.

Since our private gardens are ephemeral, we would do well to know and promote our public gardens better. Local philanthropy, volunteer efforts and national movements, such as The Garden Conservancy (www.gardenconservancy.org), need our support in Alabama.

Third, if we are astute garden travelers, like the Givhans, we will do more than enjoy the experience. We will take photographs and train our eyes. We will learn how to see, how

Birmingham Botanical Gardens' patrons Virginia and Bill Spencer

to interpret great gardens, understand their purpose and bring their secrets home.

How will we do this? Novelist Edith Wharton said it best a century ago in her classic book "Italian Villas and Their Gardens."

Here's to Alabama gardens, great and small, and the "informing spirit" they bring to all of our lives.

Jennifer Greer
January 13, 2002
Harpersville, Alabama

Jim and Elmore Inscoe of Jasmine Hill Gardens

In Search of
Great Gardens

In the spring, from a ridge atop Red Mountain, garden visitors can enjoy a view as classical as ancient Rome itself. Wild dogwood trees frame Jones Valley, with the city of Birmingham, Ala., shimmering in the distance. Along the horizon runs an arched stone wall, eclipsing neighbors' rooftops and enclosing the hilltop garden. Mounds of wild blue phlox billow like clouds around the marble bust of a Roman woman, gazing skyward.

How, you wonder, did this romantic garden with Italian Renaissance influences come to be here? The answer to this question lies in learning to see. In art and design, being able to understand what you see is the secret to enjoying it, whether the object of your attention is a fine painting or a great garden. Yet to appreciate it, you must first really see it. This requires learning several important things.

Among these are the elements of garden style. These elements include balance, scale, personality, key features and uses of plants. Great gardeners instinctively use these things to shape the garden experience and stir the emotions. Why, for example, does the blue phlox in this garden create a feeling of tranquility? Why do the horizontal lines of the wall speak of rest and calm? Why do the vertical lines of the statue stimulate the imagination? Add to this the layers of symbolism in gardens created down through the ages.

Additionally, what kind of personality do you want your garden to have? Do you enjoy the mirror-image balance, tidy lawns and neatly clipped hedges of a French parterre garden? Or do you find meaning in the winding paths and asymmetrical placements of a Japanese garden? This is not a quick decision. Look often and well, for it is pleasurable as well as instructive.

Take time to enjoy great gardens. It's the first step to bringing their secrets home.

The Spanish Courtyard

"Gardeners may feel fortunate that it was Spanish ships, which first found the way from Europe to the southern part of North America."

William C. Welch and Greg Grant, "The Southern Heirloom Garden"

RIGHT: The most famous palace in Spain, the Alhambra overlooks the city of Granada. Built by medieval Moorish sultans, the palace boasts many lovely gardens. Its Court of the Myrtles, with galleries at both ends and a mirror-like pool, emits a feeling of calm and beauty. Photograph by Ed Givhan

BELOW: The Mobile home of Palmer and Amy Hamilton is a Greek Revival structure dating from the 19th century. True to the city's roots, the Hamiltons' backyard garden has a strong Spanish influence with a gallery at one end, a classical pavilion at the other and a long, rectangular court lined with densely planted Leyland cypress. Photograph by Ed Givhan

Among the oldest traditions is the Mediterranean courtyard, which dates back to ancient Persia and Egypt, where the walled gardens of royals were irrigated oases of pools and plants in otherwise arid and barren lands. These "paradise gardens" were also favored by the Greeks, Romans and Phoenicians, and later, by invading Moors and religious orders in Spain. In Spain's hot, dry climate – with much of the land high desert – courtyards provided a welcome respite with formal pools and fountains, paved flooring, shaded galleries and potted tropical palm, fruit and olive trees.

In the 18th century, when Spain and France occupied America's northern Gulf Coast, the colonists built walled courtyards in cities such as Mobile and New Orleans. The courtyards were an excellent accommodation to the hot, humid climate, offering protection from cold in winter, shelter from heat in summer and privacy from the public on the street. In Alabama, this style can be seen at the Hotel St. James in Selma, and private gardens, such as Palmer and Amy Hamilton's and Ron and Virginia Snider's (See Chapter 2) in Mobile.

RIGHT: Influenced by Moorish builders, Spanish religious orders embraced the walled garden, as seen in the tiny town of Chinchon. Here, the Parador Nacional, a restored 16th-century convent, displays the classic features of a Spanish courtyard – a central fountain with piazza, formally arranged potted plants and a shady terrace for respite from the heat. Photograph by Ed Givhan

ABOVE: The Spanish brought the courtyard garden to Alabama, where it was also adopted by French colonists. This fusion of styles can be seen today at the Hotel St. James on the Alabama River in Selma. Local citizens restored the hotel (built in 1837), complete with a classic New Orleans-style courtyard designed by local architect Richard Hudgens. Photograph by Charlotte Hagood

Balance and Scale: Design is formal and symmetrical (mirror-image balance) and centered on a prominent water feature, scale is small and intimate

Personality: Garden is in the interior courtyard of a house or a walled enclosure abutting a structure, functions as an outdoor living space, developed in hot, semi-arid climates

Key Features: Typical features include a round/octagonal raised pool, or a sunken rectangular reflecting pool, a fountain, paved floor, and raised beds around the perimeter, a piazza, gallery or veranda that provides shady refuge

Use of Plants: Fruit trees, tropical flowers, palms and other specimen plants are in pots or raised beds, plants that fruit, flower or emit fragrance are prized.

Italian Renaissance Magic

"Some who have fallen under the spell are inclined to ascribe the Italian garden-magic to the effect of time; but, wonder-working as this undoubtedly is, it leaves many beauties unaccounted for."

Edith Wharton, *"Italian Villas and Their Gardens"*

RIGHT: The Italian Renaissance garden at Hever Castle in England was created in the early 1900s by William Waldorf Astor. With its marble statuary, evergreen plants, stone walls and classical lines, the courtyard embodies the Italian aesthetic. A 13th century moated English castle, Hever was the childhood home of Anne Boleyn and the setting for her courtship with Henry VIII. Photograph by Peggy Givhan

BELOW: The Italianate grotto at Bellingrath Gardens and Home was one of the earliest features designed by Harvard-trained landscape architect George B. Rogers in 1929. Situated atop a bluff behind the Bellingrath home, it took advantage of the natural topography. The picturesque waterfall quickly became a trademark. Photograph By Ed Givhan

Balance and Scale: Design is formal, symmetrical and well-proportioned; scale is grand, suitable for country estates

Personality: Garden is an architectural extension of the home, settings are naturalistic and romantic, often atop a hill with a view below, inspired by classical art and architecture of ancient Greece and Rome

Key Features: Water is essential; pools, waterfalls and fountains abound, as do copies of ancient architectural elements (domes, columns, arches, etc.); pergolas, grottoes, statues, vases, and other historical relics

Use of Plants: Plants substitute for architectural elements, evergreen trees serve as columns, shrubs are clipped into walls, vines are trained on pergolas to form roofs, there is minimal emphasis on flowers.

During the 15th century Italian Renaissance gardening got just the artistic inspiration – and the patrons – it needed. Wealthy Italians broke with the cloistered tradition and created expansive pleasure gardens at their country villas surrounding Rome and Florence. Undaunted by the hilly, rocky terrain, they hired architects and craftsmen to build perfectly proportioned playgrounds and elaborate outdoor rooms that were natural extensions of their homes. They were inspired by classical Roman art and literature.
In the 17th century, popular landscape painters captured these gardens on canvas and helped spread Italian Renaissance style to France and England.

Today, the lasting charm of Italian gardens springs from the union of nature, architecture and antiquities. Typical features include stone terraces and paths, Roman archways, evergreen parterres (clipped hedges planted in ornate patterns), topiary, open-air the-

ABOVE: In the 1920s and '30s, Jasmine Hill founders Benjamin and Mary Fitzpatrick made dozens of trips to Europe to commission replicas of classical Greek and Roman antiquities for their private country estate near Montgomery. Jasmine Hill's Marathon Pool – ringed by flowers and evergreen parterres – was their first major construction in the Italian Renaissance-style garden. Photograph by Ed Givhan

aters, underground grottos (caves), rooftop plantings, colonnaded loggia (open galleries), antique marble statuary, fountains, pools and cascades. (Like Alabamians, Renaissance Italians loved water.) As evidenced by visits to public places, such as Bellingrath Gardens and Home near Mobile and Jasmine Hill Gardens and Outdoor Museum in Montgomery, as well as private gardens, such as Jim Barganier's and Jim Scott's featured in Chapter 2, Italian style suits those who appreciate the finer things in life – and gardening.

RIGHT: A formal Italian-style urn and cascade overlook a small lake with fountain sprays at the Grand Hotel Marriott in Point Clear. The vintage water features – originally ornamented with Spanish tile and grillwork – date back to the 1940s and add character and elegance to the modern hotel facilities. Built in 1847, the hotel has survived – in spirit – wars, fires and hurricanes. Photograph by Jennifer Greer

French Formal

Louis XIV's "new style of gardening, much more ostentatiously flamboyant that anything seen before… swept all before it and was widely influential throughout Europe; it was perhaps the first truly international style of gardening."

Penelope Hobhouse and Patrick Taylor, "The Gardens of Europe"

RIGHT: Flower-filled parterres and a long central lawn frame France's 18th century Petite Chateau, as if it were a gem in a ring setting. Rose standards, gaura and forget-me-nots add pleasing color, and formal pathways invite strolling. Photograph by Ed Givhan

BELOW: Ed and Peggy Givhan's garden in Montgomery is a replica of a French garden near the village of Houdan in the Ile-de-France. With its geometric-shaped beds, open walls of Hetz Wintergreen arborvitae and impressive sweep of lawn, the garden complements the couple's 19th century formal Georgian-style home. Photograph by Ed Givhan

Thank Catherine de Medici of Florence for introducing her new French husband, Henri II, and his courtiers to the Italian Renaissance school of gardening. Thank the inimitable Sun King, Louis XIV, for reinventing these formal gardens on a scale the English described as "ostentatiously flamboyant."

Throughout the 17th century, French architects and engineers built vast landscapes to demonstrate the king's ability to control nature, not to mention his humble subjects. At the palace of Versailles, famed landscape architect Andre Le Nôtre created the style with its grand views, long lawns, parterres (formally-shaped beds edged with clipped evergreens,) and formal allées of trees pruned to stand like parallel rows of soldiers at attention. While the Sun King had a flair for excess, other Frenchmen scaled down the grand styles of Le Nôtre into exquisite gardens, such as the 18th century Petite Chateau in the Bagatelle Gardens, west of Paris.

French Formal style swept through Europe and was easily adapted a century later to the great plantation homes and estate gardens of the southern United States. In Alabama, the style's beauty and balance can be appreciated in the formal garden of the Greek Revival mansion of Sturdivant Hall (circa 1852) in Selma and the allée of

ABOVE: Begun in 1852, Sturdivant Hall in Selma is known as one of the finest Greek revival neo-classical antebellum mansions in the Southeast. The house is complemented by a circa 1950s, French-inspired formal garden, complete with a symmetrical layout, long center lawn, three-tiered fountain, strolling paths and enclosing parterres. Photograph by Charlotte Hagood

pecan trees at the University of Montevallo. This style also translates easily to private gardens, as evidenced by the rose garden of Claude Steele in Fairhope (see Chapter 2) and the backyard retreat of Ed and Peggy Givhan in Montgomery.

RIGHT: An example of a French allée can be seen at Flowerhill, the residence of the president of the University of Montevallo. A brick road runs through formally planted pecan trees to a Georgian mansion atop a hill. The Olmsted Brothers of Brookline, Mass., designed the campus in 1930, giving it a decidedly formal feel. Photograph by Ed Givhan

Balance and Scale: Design is formal, symmetrically balanced along a central viewing axis, frames a residence or view, geometric layout is best viewed from an elevation, scale is large and imperial, as in the residence of nobility

Personality: The effect is stately and elegant, providing a theater for strolling and feting guests (people, it's been said, were the real ornaments in the French garden), borrows elements from Italian Renaissance gardens, but displays them in a grander setting, replacing romance with magnificence

Key Features: Long rectangular lawns and strolling paths, terraces, pools, fountains, parterres, topiary, formal hedges and screens, plus allées

Use of Plants: Evergreen shrubs and trees are clipped and shaped as structure, use of flowers is restrained, except with formal accents, such as rose standards, or flowers massed for dramatic effect inside parterres.

Kitchen and Cottage Gardens

"Plants are friendly creatures and enjoy each other's company. The close-packed plants in a cottage garden grow well and look happy."

Margery Fish, "Cottage Garden Flowers"

Some things can't be improved on. Among them are the designs of traditional herb and kitchen gardens. Most date back to the 13th and 14th centuries in Europe when gardens were the medicine chests and botanical

LEFT: At Fontevrault Abbey, a restored 12th century cloister in France's Loire Valley, the kitchen garden features plants that were cultivated before 1200. Plants are set in the traditional garden layout surrounded by a "wattle," or woven wooden fence. Photograph by Ed Givhan

BELOW: The Shakespeare Garden at the Blount Cultural Park in Montgomery is true to the bard's era with its wattle fence, twig arbors, leafy bowers and thatched-roof huts. Maintained by professional gardener Karen Weber, the garden features herbs and flowers mentioned in Shakespeare's plays. Photograph by Ed Givhan

pantries of cloisters and monasteries. Monks and nuns grew medicinal plants, staple vegetables, pot herbs and prized fruits in walled settings for protection from the elements, "commoners" and animals. At France's historic Fontevrault Abbey, kitchen garden plans were simple, with geometric layouts, raised beds, wattle fences.

During the Renaissance, royalty and the well-to-do hired gardeners to develop decorative kitchen and herb gardens, or potagers, as the French called them. Meanwhile, laborers benefited from seeds, divisions and cuttings from the lord's manor, packing them tightly on a small plot of land.

The English cottage garden was once a comely mix of vegetables, herbs, roses, flowers, vines and fruit trees. Today, it is a riotous flower garden. Examples of these styles can be seen in the Shakespeare Garden in Montgomery, Grace Episcopal Church in Mt. Meigs, Arlington Antebellum Home in Birmingham, the private gardens of Fennel Mauldin, Judy Green, Laurie Dungan, Frank Fleming and Susan Lebold (see Chapter 2) and the Huntsville-Madison County Botanical Garden (see Chapter 3).

ABOVE: Grace Episcopal Church, in Mt. Meigs, Ala., is a 19th century Carpenter Gothic treasure with a garden of equal charm, thanks to Jim and Vivian Scott of Montgomery. The Scotts have surrounded the church with a Southern-style cottage garden that provides fresh flowers for the altar. Photograph by Ed Givhan

ABOVE: At Arlington Home and Gardens in Birmingham, a straight brick pathway and formal beds set the scene for an exuberant kitchen and cutting garden. Maintained by professional gardener Sharon Odom, the beds are packed with vegetables on one side and with herbs and old fashioned flowers on the other. Photograph by Charlotte Hagood

Kitchen Gardens

Balance and scale: Designs are formal, symmetrical with four-square and six-square layouts, raised beds and well-defined paths; scale can be small or grand

Personality: Evolving from cloister gardens of the Middle Ages, either hidden from view or on display, tidiness rules

Key Features: Gardens are fenced, trellises add height for climbing vegetables, accents include armillary, sundials, benches, shady arbors

Use of plants: Beds are filled with herbs, vegetables, small fruits, medicinal plants, and edible flowers, planted in rows.

Cottage Gardens

Balance and Scale: Designs combine formal structure with wildly informal plantings, scale is small

Personality: Plants are closely spaced, re-seeding plants and rambling forms invite a mix of colors and textures

Key Features: Flowers are essential, gardens are fenced, with little or no lawn; obelisks, arbors and trellises give height to vines and roses; potted plants abound

Use of plants: Favorites include old-fashioned roses, flowering shrubs and small trees, climbing vines, reseeding annuals, bulbs, bedding plants, long-lived perennials.

Colonial Style

"I can truly say that I'd rather be at home at Mount Vernon with a friend or two about me, than to be attended at the seat of the government by the officers of state and representatives of every power in Europe."

George Washington, *private journal*

ABOVE & RIGHT: The tranquil courtyard, above, at the Conde-Charlotte House in Mobile illustrates the type of garden retreat favored by the Spanish when their flag flew over the city from 1780 to 1813. Created by the Colonial Dames in the 1950s, the walled garden enjoys a four-square layout, evergreen parterres and a central Spanish-tiled fountain. It is similar in feeling to the carefully restored William Paca House garden, at right, built in colonial Annapolis, Md. This 18th century garden also features a formal geometric layout, neatly clipped parterres, a central focal point and walls for privacy. Photographs by Ed Givhan

LEFT: The Southern Living Colonial Garden captures the flavor of the period at the American Village civic education center in Montevallo. The formal pleasure garden features evergreen parterres full of annual bedding plants that change with the seasons (a modern convenience). The village and garden are modeled after Mt. Vernon, George and Martha Washington's plantation in Virginia. Photo by Jennifer Greer

Amid the chaos of settlement and revolution, Southern colonists turned to their gardens for touchstones with the familiar and stable. They borrowed geometry and order from formal European gardens, especially France, but simplified their designs with local plants, materials and democratic tastes.

A colonial city garden, such as the two-acre, walled "pleasure garden" at the William Paca House in Annapolis, Md., bespoke the prosperity and sophistication of its owner (a wealthy planter and signer of the Declaration of Independence). Pioneer or rural gardens relied on the traditional four-square layout for herbs, vegetables, fruits and flowers.

Over time, this tradition appeared in the country pleasure and flower gardens popular in the South, such as the French Colonial Maison Chenal near St.

Francisville, La. On large colonial plantations, such as George Washington's Mount Vernon, Va., Southerners created model farms complete with rolling meadows, wooded parks, kitchen gardens, pleasure gardens, orchards and botanical collections. In Alabama today, we can see examples of colonial style in

the courtyard at the Conde-Charlotte House in Mobile, the country garden at Petals from the Past nursery in Jemison and the pleasure garden at American Village in Montevallo. Colonial influences also emerge in private gardens, such as Louise Wrinkle's courtyard garden (see Chapter 2.)

Balance and Scale: Design is formal and geometric, placement of beds and paths is symmetrical and perfectly balanced, scale is adaptable, from small and intimate to the size of a city block and imposing

Personality: Inspired by European garden styles of the 15th to 17th centuries, city gardens are an extension of the house; sophisticated, often walled for privacy and used for entertaining, homestead gardens are utilitarian, set apart from the house, and fenced for protection from animals; plantation gardens are extensive, a series of pleasure and kitchen gardens, botanical collections, greenhouses and arboreta spread across a planned landscape

Key Features: Strong emphasis on paths (stone, brick or gravel), a center ornament (fountain, tree or sculpture, etc.), parterres, well-defined areas of lawn, hedges or fences; pleasure gardens are placed near the house for viewing from a window, porch or veranda

Use of Plants: Evergreen plants, such as boxwood or privet, are clipped as hedges to edge parterres; trees and shrubs are often natives; period plants include roses, daffodils, pinks, hollyhocks, lilies, daises, hyacinths and herbs, such as oregano, lavender, thyme and rosemary

LEFT: Maison Chenal, outside of St. Francisville, La., is a restored French Colonial Country house with a wrap-around porch for viewing the pleasure garden. Key features include the formal evergreen parterres (in common privet) laid out in geometric patterns and outlined with gravel strolling paths and a picket fence.

BELOW: Alabama nurseryman Jason Powell acheives a similar look with his old-fashioned display garden, Petals from the Past in Jemison. Starting with a raised cottage and wraparound porch, he added a traditional, four-square layout to display heirloom plants, a parterre-patterned lawn and fenced enclosure. Photographs by Ed Givhan

Plantation and Estate Gardens

"At the Bellingrath Gardens entrance, plant life suddenly becomes ordered and Southern hospitality gushes profusely … France may have Versailles, the legacy of its Sun King. Alabama has Bellingrath Gardens, the legacy of a soft-drink (Coke) bottler."

Chicago Tribune

In the early 19th century, as the state prospered, well-to-do Alabamians began to view the garden as a calling card for Southern hospitality. Antebellum plantation owners and wealthy merchants maintained elaborate formal gardens as evidence of social refinement. Among those preserving vintage garden traditions today are preservationists at Gaineswood in Demopolis, the Battle-Friedman House in Tuscaloosa and Arlington Antebellum Home and Gardens in Birmingham.

In the early 20th century, during what some call "the golden age of gardening" in America, Alabama saw the creation of another legacy when two wealthy couples built private country estates. One of them is now an internationally known tourist destination – Bellingrath Gardens and Home, south of Mobile. The other is the romantic Jasmine Hill Gardens and Outdoor Museum, near Montgomery. Today, owners of private historic homes often research period gardens and restore or re-create them to com-plete the picture of gracious living. Among these is the parterre garden at Pleasant Ridge (circa 1840), near Camden, now the home of Jimmy and Ginger Stewart. In this modern age, when lawns are too often confused with landscapes, ball fields called parks, and condos billed as hotels, elegance still has a place.

RIGHT: Jimmy and Ginger Stewart of Canton Bend, west of Camden, benefit from the foresight of former owners of the historic Bethea-Strother-Stewart home. In the late 1980s, a French-style boxwood parterre was installed as a side garden. Its formal personality complements the modified Georgian-style house, which is on the National Historic Register. Photograph by Ed Givhan

LEFT: "Girl Playing Knuckle Bones" (an ancient game of dice) is a marble copy of an original in the British Museum. The Hellenistic statue adds a grace note to what was once the country estate garden of Benjamin and Mary Fitzpatrick. Jasmine Hill is now a public garden and an outdoor museum. Photograph by Ed Givhan

BELOW: Kiss-me-by-the-gate (winter honeysuckle) is one of the old-fashioned shrubs that dots the landscape at Gaineswood. Preservationists are working to enhance the antebellum boxwood gardens. Photograph by Ed Givhan

Balance and Scale:
Designs are hybrids of
classic European tradi-
tions, blending geomet-
ric and curvilinear lay-
outs, mixing formal
structures with informal
plantings; scale is grand,
as in a country estate or
plantation

Personality: Gardens
reflect prosperous times
and period fashions:
antebellum Southern
hospitality, Victorian fascination with cottage
flowers and tropical
plants, or the Roaring
20s' attraction to roman-
tic themes

Key Features: Extensive
lawns, boxwood parter-
res, formal allées, foun-
tains, pools, statuary,
plazas, bridges, gaze-
bos, lakes and summer
houses

Use of Plants: Long-
lived trees, shrubs and
bulbs are true to the
original landscape,
newer plants were
added in later genera-
tions, today each is a
showplace of horticultur-
al fashion and seasonal
change

ABOVE: In the 1840s, a prominent Tuscaloosa
planter's wife, Millicent Battle, commissioned an
English-Empire style "strolling garden" at the
Battle-Friedman House museum on Greensboro
Avenue. Restoration will incorporate historically
accurate antebellum plants, plus Victorian favorites,
such as geraniums, begonias and caladiums.
Photograph by Charlotte Hagood

ABOVE: Arlington Antebellum Home & Gardens
includes a variety of colorful period gardens planted behind and along the sides of the Greek
Revival mansion. Among them are showy examples of Victorian-style "carpet bedding" – flowers
mass in ornate fashion to resemble exotic carpets
– like this raised bed full of bold, bronzed cannas
planted in a sea of creeping Jenny. Photograph by
Jennifer Greer

Landscape Parks

"True wit is nature to advantage dressed, What oft was thought but ne're so well expressed."

Alexander Pope, Essay on Criticism

ABOVE: Begun in 1743, Stourhead is one of the greatest English landscape parks. Tons of dirt were moved, a river was diverted and damned up, and trees were cut and replanted – all to acquire the perfect pastoral effect. Classical architecture, such as an aqueduct, and spring blooming trees add to the Virgilian ideal. Photograph by Ed Givhan

RIGHT: At Bellingrath Gardens, a rustic bridge arches gently over Mirror Lake, created in the late 1920s. Framed by water and woodlands, the scene reflects the picturesque English tradition. In the summer and fall, blooms from yellow allamanda cast a yellow glow over the bridge, while the natural woodlands create a soft, romantic canopy. Photograph by Ed Givhan

Balance and Scale:
Layouts are asymmetrical and informal, scale is grand, suitable for large country estates and parks, and more recently, country clubs, golf courses, college campus and other public grounds

Personality: Picturesque scenes inspired by romantic 18th century landscape paintings of the ancient Italian countryside, nourished by the English love of nature, interest in classical architecture and desire to break with French formality

Key Features: An expansive vista to be viewed from the residence and/or the approach to it; winding trails that reveal carefully arranged scenes with rounded hills, groves of trees, park-like woods, expanses of lawn; lakes and rivers, accented with classical bridges, ruins or temples

Use of Plants: Native trees, shrubs and herbaceous plants, plus some exotic specimens with natural appeal, lawn grasses.

By the 18th century, politics, economics and fashion joined forces in a strong English reaction against elaborate French geometry and parterres. Englishmen, such as Lancelot "Capability" Brown, championed a more natural style of gardening, one that enhances the "capabilities" of the land. Known as English landscape gardens or parks, these were large picturesque settings like the great Stourhead, near Bath. Of paramount importance was that they did not appear contrived by the hand of man. (Never mind that every hill, dale, lake and Roman bridge was carefully designed, constructed and maintained.)

Subsequently, American men of the land – Thomas Jefferson, Andrew Jackson Downing and Frederick Law Olmsted – took up the cause of the picturesque landscape, and experts say it has had the most lasting impact of any style in our public consciousness. (Check out the scaled-down version in the front lawn of any subdivision.) In

ABOVE: The English-inspired design for the 300-acre Blount Cultural Park in Montgomery was among the last major projects completed by London's celebrated landscape architect Russell Page. Among Page's many contributions was to site the Carolyn Blount Theater atop a hill. It is the first thing visitors see after passing through an allée of tulip poplars. Photograph by Ed Givhan

TOP: Legendary architect Robert Trent Jones Sr. took advantage of the "capability" of the Alabama landscape when he designed an award-winning golf trail for the Retirement Systems of Alabama. At the Capitol Hill course near Prattville, it's possible to tee off in the foothills of the Appalachians and continue playing in the Coastal Plain – as long as your ball doesn't wind up in the Alabama River. Photograph by Ed Givhan

Alabama, English park-like landscapes can be enjoyed at Bellingrath Gardens near Mobile, the Blount Cultural Park in Montgomery and the Capitol Hill Golf Course in Prattville.

English Naturalistic Style

"The brilliancy was beyond anything we had seen in the way of hardy flowers…. The great point in this border is the grouping of colors in broad masses…. It is this soft and insensible transition from one mass of color to another that is so effective…."

Gertrude Jekyll, "The Garden"

In the late 19th and early 20th centuries, the English, or naturalistic, garden came into full glory, creating a romantic vision of the garden that continues to inspire. Originally, these gardens were characterized by formal structure – such as a series of garden rooms, often enclosed by clipped boxwood, hedges or masonry walls – softened by lush, informal plantings. Later designs include winding paths and curvilinear shapes.

Inspired by a Victorian fascination with flowers, English-style gardens were promoted by British garden designers, such as William Robinson, Gertrude Jekyll and Vita-Sackville West. Among the highlights of the English garden were complex herbaceous borders woven with hundreds of flowers,

RIGHT: There are few public places in Alabama where English style succeeds on such a grand scale as it does at the Huntsville-Madison County Botanical Garden. In the Central Corridor Garden, a series of deep flower borders runs the long axis of a strolling lawn. The garden consulted with noted Southern plant expert Allan Armitage in the selection of more than 300 varieties for the borders. Photograph by Charlotte Hagood

LEFT: Threave Castle, a 19th century manor house owned by Scotland's National Trust, is home to the country's National Gardening School. Among the 80 acres planted by students is a particularly lovely English-style garden, set in an emerald sward of clipped lawn and framed by mature trees. Stone walls – lined with lushly planted beds – enclose the garden. Photograph by Ed Givhan

RIGHT: Considering Claude Monet's naturalistic garden in Giverny, France, it's easy to see where the artist drew inspiration for some of his most famous paintings. Monet was keenly interested in the effects of light on the landscape. His garden allowed him to explore many themes, including water lillies. Photograph by Ed Givhan

BELOW: At the Huntsville-Madison County Botanical Garden, an Oriental gallery acts as a bridge over the Aquatic Garden. Typical of English style, the formal structure is surrounded by lush, informal plantings and a grove of mature trees. It almost seems to float on the surface of the pond. Photograph by Charlotte Hagood

herbs, grasses, vines and shrubs to create four-season interest. This was no small feat. One of Miss Jekyll's borders was 200 feet long and 14 feet wide! Today, examples of English, or naturalistic, style can be seen all over Europe, including the romantic Threave Castle in Scotland and Claude Monet's suitably impressionistic garden in Giverny, France. Closer to home, the English garden can be enjoyed all over the state, but especially at the Huntsville-Madison County Botanical Garden, as well as prvate gardens, such as Ira Mitchell's and Susan Lebold's in Birmingham (See Chapter 2.)

Balance and Scale: Early examples are formal garden rooms often enclosed by hedges or walls, softened by lush, informal plantings; contemporary designs include more curvilinear lines and paths; scale adapts to any size

Personality: Originated on Britain's country estates, influences include English landscape parks, Impressionist paintings and an Edwardian attraction to cottage flowers; gardens used for strolling and pleasure

Key Features: Paths or lawns lined with sumptuous flower and shrub borders, clipped evergreen hedges, masonry walls, formal pools, classical statues, vine-covered arbors, Chippendale benches, swings and park-like woods

Use of Plants: Herbaceous borders brim with a seasonal succession of hardy perennials, biennials, old-fashioned seed-grown annuals and long-blooming bedding plants, with small trees, shrubs and vines for year-round interest

ABOVE & LEFT: With its weeping willows, loose flower borders, water lilies and a reflecting pond, this scene from the Aquatic Garden in Huntsville is reminiscent of Monet's garden at Giverny. Summer raindrops puddle the pond's surface and echo the shape of lily pads, while two bronze cranes refresh themselves. Photograph by Jennifer Greer

Contemporary Public Gardens

"A modest garden contains, for those who know how to look and to wait, more instruction than a library."

Henri Frederic Amiel, private journal

ABOVE: In the spring, all paths lead to discovery in the Kaul Wildflower Garden at the Birmingham Botanical Gardens. Noted for its extensive collection of wildflowers, native shrubs and trees, the garden is located on the site of an old rock quarry. Photograph by Jennifer Greer

The search for great gardens ultimately leads to contemporary public gardens, and what fitting destinations they are in Alabama. These gardens showcase a wide variety of garden styles and represent important collections of botanical wealth, art and architecture. They become favorite places to visit with the family, or hike, birdwatch or meditate by oneself. Public gardens also serve as outdoor classrooms for horticulture, landscape design and ecology. As such, they create the nucleus of the modern gardening community, attracting dedicated hobbyists, professionals, universi-

ty extension agents, garden club members and Master Gardeners for a constant exchange of information and ideas.

Central Alabama is lucky to have the Birmingham Botanical Gardens, the Charles Ireland Sculpture Garden at the Birmingham Museum of Art, Ecoscape at Birmingham Southern College, the new Aldridge Gardens in Hoover and the Arboretum at the University of Alabama in Tuscaloosa. Farther north, major educational gardens include the Huntsville-Madison County Botanical Garden and the new tropical garden at the Anniston Museum of Natural History. In Mobile and Dothan, newer botanical gardens reflect the strong gardening interest in South Alabama, already rich in horticultural history. As the state urbanizes in the 21st century, public botanical gardens will provide an increasingly vital link between Alabama's rural past and its cultural and ecological future.

LEFT: The "Tree Topology" walk at the University of Alabama Arboretum takes students more than 40 feet up in the air to the canopy to learn about ecology and natural history. Northport blacksmith Steve Davis created the ornamental gate. Photograph by Jennifer Greer

BELOW: Students at the Alabama School for the Blind learn about plants from touch, smell, taste and Braile signs. Handrails make navigating easy. This special garden was created by local members of the Garden Clubs of America. Photograph by Jennifer Greer

BELOW: With its ageless and maternal lines, a weathered boulder is reflected in the lake's waters at the Birmingham Botanical Gardens. In a Japanese garden, boulders such as this one are placed carefully, representing stability in an ever-changing world. Photograph by Charlotte Hagood

ABOVE: The winding path garden – created to alternately hide and reveal the surrounding landscape – is a traditional concept in Japanese design. When the cherry trees and azaleas bloom in Spring at the Birmingham Botanical Gardens' Japanese Gardens, the path beckons with equal parts charm and mystery. Photograph by Jennifer Greer

"The flow of the river — whatever I compare it to leaves out the stones on the bottom."
Tawara Machi, "Salad Anniversary"

ABOVE: The traditional goal of Japanese garden design is to re-create the character of the larger natural landscape in a microcosm. In Birmingham, local architect Darcey Tatum worked with Masaji "Buffy" Murai, a Japanese architect from St. Louis, to create the Japanese Gardens in the late 1960s. Photograph by Charlotte Hagood

LEFT: Rodin's "Jean D'Aire" creates a powerful presence in the Charles W. Ireland Sculpture Garden at the Birmingham Museum of Art. With its large shade trees, iron benches and contemplative "Blues Pools Courtyard," the garden is an oasis of green in the city's center. The plaza and pools are the work of Mississippi native Valerie Jaudon. Photographs by Charlotte Hagood

"A garden will move us to the extent that it engages the imagination as well as the senses."
Michael Pollan, "Second Nature"

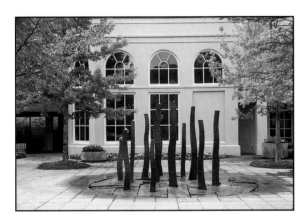

LEFT: "The Granite Garden," a sculptue by Jesus Bautista Moroles, provides striking vertical interest and a glistening water feature near the entrance of the Birmingham Botanical Gardens. The plaza is lined with native Shumard oaks. Photograph by Jennifer Greer

BELOW: At the Anniston Museum of Natural History, the Courtyard Garden's unique design creates an ideal microclimate for tropical plants and other exotics, including cannas, ferns, cycads, bananas and the largest outdoor collection of palms in Alabama. The metal sculpture, "Motion," is the work of Mark Lane and functions as a fountain. Photograph by Charlotte Hagood

"Nature's places, no matter how beautiful and moving … are not yet gardens; they become gardens only when shaped by our actions and engaged by our dreams."

William Turnbull, Jr.
"The Poetics of Gardens"

RIGHT: Designed by local landscape architect Alexander Vare, EcoScape cuts a striking form in an area that was once a dump. This New American garden was established in 1996 on the campus of Birmingham-Southern College under the direction of Roald Hazelhoff, director of BSC's Southern Environmental Center. Photograph by Jennifer Greer

BELOW: While it's a contemporary garden, EcoScape draws on ancient aesthetics and concepts with its upright stone walls, naturalistic plantings and sundial. Created by Dennis Hunt and Arthur Price, the sundial sculpture is one of many pieces of original artwork that also instruct. Photograph by Jennifer Greer

ABOVE: An outdoor class-
room, EcoScape teaches
new gardening practices,
including xeriscaping and
water conservation, to
schools and communities.
A butterfly border – full of
Mexican sage, lantana,
cleome, rudbeckia and butterfly bush tells the story of
these important and lovely
pollinators. Photograph by
Jennifer Greer

ABOVE: A nearby, giant Praying Mantis sculpture, the work
of Allen Peterson, helps children understand the importance of beneficial insects. Photograph by Jennifer Greer

Behind the
Garden Gates

In our search for gardens, great and small, we discovered many unique and wonderful places. Along Mobile Bay, Claude Steele grows his favorite roses and vegetables in a charming Victorian setting. In Safford, Ed and Peggy Givhan enjoy a country flower garden that would have made their grandmothers proud. In Montgomery, Jim Barganier takes pleasure in his own Italian villa. In Birmingham, Weesie Smith makes a beautiful case for ecology gardening. At Lake Martin, Jim Scott designs the ultimate pleasure garden. In Cullman, Calera McHenry grows herbs for health and happiness. In Anniston, Hayes Jackson is growing tropical plants well north of the frost line. In Florence, Maria Wall has carved a fantasy in moss.

Each of the 22 gardens featured here makes a statement about the gardener – his or her values, sense of history, connections to family, and feelings about the land. Some gardeners start with an interest in plants and develop a garden to accommodate their collections. Others start with a dream and search out plants and other materials with which to build it. Still others start with a love of place and seek to enhance or restore it. As a result, the gardens include a variety of styles – formal and informal, traditional and contemporary, stylized and individualistic. They also reflect Alabama's diverse landscape, from the Gulf Coast to the Black Belt, from the Ridges and Valleys to the Piedmont, from the Tennessee Valley to the Appalachian Mountains.

Most of these gardens are private retreats, and we thank the gardeners for sharing them with us for our book. You will find gardens like them in your neighborhoods, among friends in garden clubs and plant societies, and on springtime home and garden tours. Seek them out. Turn off the how-to TV for a while, and go behind Alabama's garden gates. See the inspired hand of real gardeners at work. In the end, that's what makes a garden great.

ABOVE: True to the spirit of Italian Renaissance style, Jim's garden acts as an architectural extension of the house. Faced with an odd triangular-shaped space, he enhanced the proportions with a checker-board lawn of paving squares and zoysia grass.

RIGHT: Jim Barganier and his architectural firm have several claims to fame, including Montgomery's Museum of Fine Arts. Yet one of his most impressive feats, in the eyes of neighbors, is the Roman villa he created from a re-modeled 1940s ranch house.

RIGHT: Jim transformed a concrete urn into a fountain by notching the rim and using the piece to recirculate the water in the pool.

Viva la Villa
Montgomery

PHOTOGRAPHY BY ED GIVHAN

A fan of the great Italian Renaissance architect Andrea Palladio, Montgomery architect Jim Barganier frequently lectures on this design style – when he's not enjoying his own Roman villa. Several years ago, Jim surprised residents of the Edgewood Plantation area when he bought a 1940s red brick ranch house and announced plans to remodel it. (Jim likes challenges. He had already restored Edgewood, a 1821 Federal-style residence that is possibly Montgomery's oldest house.) Today, his transformed ranch house and landscape embody the Italian Renaissance, with characteristic playfulness, sensuality and architectural harmony. The stage is set with a long gallery of Tuscan columns across

ABOVE: Old French gates open to the pool, where a contemporary obelisk (designed by the owner) casts its reflection in the water. This contemplative scene can be viewed from a guest room.

Jim Barganier

the house's newly white facade. Around back, a dazzling checkerboard patio opens to a private courtyard with a swimming pool. Enclosing the area are the house, a white brick wall and yet another colonnade. A 12-foot hedge of tightly planted Thuja Hetz Wintergreen forms a boundary on each end of the pool. The tall, columnar arborvitae afford yet another Italian accent, as do a cluster of clay olive jars, an original urn-shaped fountain and a 15-foot tall obelisk. Where did Jim get the inspiration for such a garden? He and his wife, Jane, spent their honeymoon in Italy and southern France, and fell in love with classical styles. Viva la villa.

ABOVE: Bill and Linda Brock enjoy working together in their garden. He builds the structures. She plants the plants.

RIGHT: Bill's stone retaining walls and curving, mulched paths showcase the native woods and Linda's natural plantings.

INSET: One of the few ferns that can take some sun, Southern shield is at home with purple coneflower.

Woodland Sanctuary
Gardendale

PHOTOGRAPHY BY JENNIFER GREER
AND CHARLOTTE HAGOOD

BELOW: A stone-walled pond provides an area for wildlife watching in the sunny area between the woods and the house.

During Alabama's summers, few places are as cool and soul soothing as a private woodland retreat. Just ask Linda and Bill Brock of Gardendale. The Brocks live in a residential neighborhood north of Birmingham in the ridges and valleys that mark the last ripple of the Appalachian Mountains. Their house sits atop a hill, and behind it, a scenic hardwood forest drops into a ravine filled with moss-covered rocks, ferns and lush native vegetation. The steep, wooded site would have been difficult to landscape. Instead, the Brocks used the forest as a backdrop for native and naturalistic plantings. Along the brow of the hill, they carved a path that created a safe, easy view of the woods on one side. On the other side, raised beds display an extensive collection of ferns and wildflowers. Where the plantings transition to a sunny lawn, a small pond (with handsome stone walls) attracts birds, butterflies, frogs and other wildlife. Sitting on a nearby bench in the shade of a magnolia tree, you learn the simple truth about the Brocks' garden. What began as an oasis for nature has become a sanctuary for the human spirit.

ABOVE: A bumblebee is attracted to native Joe Pye weed, also a summer favorite of butterflies.

French Provincial
Montgomery

PHOTOGRAPHY BY ED GIVHAN
AND CHARLOTTE HAGOOD

ABOVE: The view from Catherine and Robert Cope's kitchen window looks like a scene out of a French travel book.

Several years ago, Catherine and Robert Cope set out to create a garden around their newly built house on old pastureland in rural Montgomery County. Today, in a testament to what two passionate gardeners can accomplish, they enjoy a French provincial garden as charming as any in Normandy. Luxuriant flower gardens surround the period house, which is approached by a straight stone walkway. Stroll past drifts of ginger lilies, daylilies, salvia, daisy and veronica, which overflow their beds to partially conceal the formal structure. The design frames a series of views that give meaning to the chaos of blooms, create a serene haven and lead to outdoor living areas. Smaller stone paths wind through the garden, drawing the eye into each new vignette – a hedge of pink shrub roses, an elegant ceramic pot or an intimate seating area. Inside the house, every window and French door affords a framed view of the naturalistic garden, which was inspired, in part, by garden travel. "We have been to Giverny and seen how it vibrated with energy, but we went to France after we created the garden," says Catherine, with a chuckle. "This is really our personal garden, a blend of English style and French romanticism, using Southern plants that we have found grow well here." Whether you are in this garden, or looking out on it, the Copes' creation offers something very necessary these days – the joy of living, or as the French say, *joie de vivre*.

ABOVE: Catherine, an artist, is always creating nooks and niches in the garden. Robert loves to grow woodland ferns, ornamental grasses and experiment with wildflowers in the field.

RIGHT: In back, the Copes have preserved the pastoral view. An evergreen hedge defines the near horizon, while an expanse of grass sweeps down to a lake shared by the Milly Branch community.

BELOW: The Copes commissioned an architect to design a French provincial house, which they surrounded with personal flower gardens.

45

ABOVE: An inveterate propagator, Tom grafted this May-blooming Kousa dogwood – and seven others – from a single cutting that an Arkansas woman sent him in the mail.

ABOVE: Cannon's Double, a hybrid of the Alabama native Austrinum azalea, glows like embers in late April.

April in Loachapoaka
Loachapoaka

PHOTOGRAPHY BY TOM CORLEY, ED GIVHAN AND JENNIFER GREER

OPPOSITE PAGE: In the woods around Corley's Cabin, the gardener grows 475 species of rhododendrons, such as this *Roseum* elegans, a popular hybrid.

April is a big event in Loachapoaka, a tiny village west of Auburn in the rolling Piedmont countryside. To find out why, turn off Lee County 64 at a special sign for Corley's Cabin, and enter an 18-acre private woodland. Shafts of sunlight penetrate the forest, revealing a wonderland of color – reds, pinks, whites, yellows, oranges, magentas, purples – in the understory shrubs. This is the garden of Tom Corley, a veteran collector and grower. His woods are home to 475 rhododendrons, more than 1,500 native and hybrid azaleas, a collection of 10 rare dogwoods, more than 1,000 camellias, and many other blooming trees and shrubs. Tom is a retired associate director of the Agricultural Experiment Station and associate dean of the College of Agriculture at Auburn University. He and his wife, Mary, live in Auburn, but Tom spends a lot of time at his cabin, where he greets visitors passing through on garden tours of the Deep South. "When I first moved here 20 years ago, I found several dozen Piedmont azaleas (*Rhododendron canescens*) in the woods," he recalls. "I collected the seed and found out I could grow them easily. The blooms are beautiful, and I never know what kind of surprise I'm going to get." With some of the South's loveliest native and ornamental trees and shrubs blooming almost year-round, every day brings a surprise at Corley's Cabin.

ABOVE: At the end of the road sits a lovingly restored pioneer log cabin that Tom moved from near his home in Coosa County.

ABOVE: A member of the Chattahoochee Chapter of the American Society of Rhododendrons, Tom Corley swaps seeds of natives and hybrids with other azalea aficionados South.

Quintessential Cottage
Mobile

PHOTOGRAPHY BY Ed Givhan

"The tiniest garden is often the loveliest. Look at our cottage gardens, if you need to be convinced." That advice comes to us from Vita Sackville-West, the great English gardener and stylist who championed the unpretentious flower gardens of the 19th century working class. Vita would have been inspired by the exquisite cottage garden of Laurie and Rotch Dungan on Glenwood Street in Mobile. When the Dungans first moved into their 1928 Arts-and-Crafts-era cottage, Laurie took one look at the four overgrown azalea bushes around the house and started planting flowers. Today, most of her lot is given over to flowers, herbs and foliage plants, with only a little lawn. A New Dawn climbing rose crowns the front door. Potted plants cluster around the steps. Pansies and violas spill into walkways. Hanging petunias dangle over raised beds. Laurie credits part of her "green thumb" to the muscle power of her husband, Rotch (a teacher, high school football coach and builder of raised garden beds). While she started gardening as a hobbyist, Laurie now works as a garden designer and landscaper. As charming as her garden, she blushes at the suggestion that she has one of the prettiest cottage gardens around. "That's the sweetest thing anybody ever said to me," Laurie protests. But the pictures tell the story.

BELOW: Laurie and Rotch Dungan enjoy an afternoon in the garden with Virginia Givhan, the author's granddaughter and part-time photo assistant.

ABOVE: How does Laurie get that exuberant look in her flower borders? Raised beds – filled with plenty of enriched soil – offer the plants superior drainage and excellent growing conditions in hot, humid Mobile.

LEFT: Laurie likes to plant old-fashioned, easy-care annuals and perennials, such as daisies, phlox, iris, lamb's ear, verbena, petunia, pansies and violas. Neighborhood children say her cottage garden "looks like a fairy tale." She lets them pick flowers whenever they want.

Garden of Earthly Delights
Homewood

PHOTOGRAPHY BY JENNIFER GREER
AND CHARLOTTE HAGOOD

LEFT: The artist gives his exuberant cottage garden enough structure in the way of paths, beds, walls and decks that visitors don't get lost.

ABOVE: "In my studio, I have to have control. In my garden, I'm not in control. I like working with nature and not having control over it," says the artist and gardener.

OPPOSITE PAGE: Frank Fleming's sculptures of nature spirits hearken to his childhood in Bear Creek, Ala., when animals were among his best friends.

51

ABOVE: Frank's naturalistic sculptures are as at home in the garden as they are in museums all over the country.

A visit to Frank Fleming's hillside garden is a journey into the imagination. Here, as no where else, the artist's memories of growing up on a farm in the Tennessee Valley merge with his witty, contemporary visions of nature. While

ABOVE: Oriental lilies, wonderfully fragrant, are the artist's passion.

Frank is recognized as an award-winning sculptor, he says he's just "a pure Alabama redneck boy" in the garden. Clad in a T-shirt, sneakers and shorts, he scrambles up steep front steps, leading guests past well-crafted terraces and raised beds. On one side, a richly textured conifer garden creates a gallery for some of his larger bronze pieces – while walling off an uninviting view of the neighbors' rooftops. On the opposite side sits a vegetable and flower garden, with the beds full of good, imported topsoil and lots of manure. Behind his modest bungalow, the "yard" features a weathered deck and an old-fashioned cottage garden full of favorites, such as poppies, money plant, larkspur, pinks, iris, daisies, purple coneflower and lilies. On one side, the deck is defined by tin-and-wooden wall with crude windows, reminiscent of an old farm shack. Before you leave, Frank presses a jar of homemade fig preserves into your hands. It's a good thing. Were it not for the delicious physical evidence to carry home, you would think you had spent the afternoon in a dream.

LEFT Giant alliums, oriental lilies and delphinium lend a surrealistic mood to the vegetable garden.

OPPOSITE PAGE: On the back deck, a rustic wall, a window-framing view and a muscadine vine bespeak Alabama country.

Country Revival
Safford

PHOTOGRAPHY BY ED GIVHAN AND CHARLOTTE HAGOOD

The first spring after Ed and Peggy Givhan bought an old family farmhouse near Safford in Dallas County, they noticed something wonderful happening. Yellow daffodils sprang up, followed by hyacinths, columbine, white iris, spider lilies and other old-fashioned flowers. They learned that the original owner, Betty Givhan, had been an avid gardener. Ed and Peggy realized immediately that they had inherited dozens of heirloom flowers and ornamental plants, which they called "Messages from Miss Betty." Ed and Peggy not only restored the house to its original charm, they recreated an Alabama country garden based on memories of their grandmothers' gardens and research of Southern garden history. "In rural Alabama, our grandmothers created their gardens with inexpensive, seed-grown flowers, such as zinnia, cleome and cosmos, interspersed with a few prized perennials, such as iris and columbine," says Ed. "Victorian structures – fences, pillars, planters – bestowed form and order." If ever a garden has a sense of place, so lovingly revived for a new generation, it's this one.

ABOVE: Ed and Peggy Givhan have sought to define the best of old and new methods of growing Southern flowers.

LEFT: One reason that the Givhans' garden is successful is because it takes advantage of the sense of place provided by views of the Black Belt farmland.

BELOW: The future of a family farm cottage was in jeopardy when Ed and Peggy saved it. They surrounded the Victorian house with a fitting country garden.

Naturescape
Tuscaloosa/Northport

PHOTOGRAPHY BY JENNIFER GREER
AND CHARLOTTE HAGOOD

In Northport, Adrian and Betty Jo Goldstein enjoy the best of both gardening worlds. They built their home on a tranquil wooded lot with a good bit of natural slope. They

ABOVE: "I just enjoy being outdoors and experimenting with plants" says Adrian Goldstein, a Master Gardener, in his naturalistic garden with his wife, Betty Jo.

wanted to save the big hardwood trees on the site, so they started out with a dense shade garden. About eight years ago, Adrian "saw the light" and cleared a stand of pine trees in the woods. Today, shady woods for planting hosta, ferns, spring-blooming wildflowers and shrubs surround them. They now have ample sun for a water garden and raised stone beds full of spring and summer bulbs, perennial flowers and grasses. Yet the most impressive feature of this garden is its success at marrying the wood-frame house with a naturally beautiful site. The approach to the residence is a winding drive though park-like woods. Inside the house, a picture window looks out on a rock-ledged water garden. Through open windows, you can hear the sound of falling water. Outside, a wooden deck follows a man-made stream to a screened, summerhouse that catches the breeze in the trees. This isn't simply landscaping. It's naturescaping.

ABOVE: A landscape architect helped Adrian design a rock pool that is the centerpiece of the garden design.

ABOVE: A sunny clearing created opportunities for a collection of old-fashioned bulbs such as crocosmia, which spills over raised stone beds.

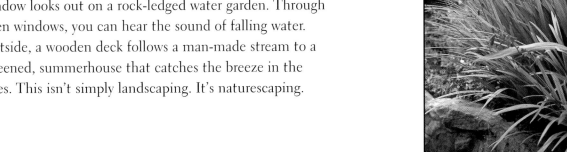

OPPOSITE PAGE: By saving the large hardwoods, the Goldsteins preserved the integrity of the site and created a shade garden. INSET: At treetop level, the summerhouse is a great place to read or catch an afternoon nap.

Courtyard Show
Montgomery

PHOTOGRAPHY BY ED GIVHAN

ABOVE: A three-foot-tall raised bed – made from concrete block covered with stucco – sets the stage for Bill Gordy's three-season flower show. It's easily viewed from the patio or the interior of the house.

Bill Gordy's garden never looks the same two years in a row. Like the director of a successful Broadway theater, Bill constantly searches for the next hit border, the next star plant and the next audience to enjoy his courtyard garden.

ABOVE: Bill Gordy, who recently turned 80, loves to share. If you're a gardening friend, and there are many, he's happy to root a plant for you, or provide flowers for weddings, parties and funerals.

Bill understands how to create a first-class show. One of the best examples is the lavish English-style flower border that he plants each spring in an attractive, stucco raised bed. The 50-foot-long, three-foot-high bed not only displays the flower border along the viewing line, it puts the performers at eye level. Let's face it – when a chorus line of foxglove and poppies is head high, it gets your attention. What's more, Bill's Mediterranean-style courtyard maximizes beauty and minimizes maintenance. Potted plants adorn tables and corners. Vines drape the walls. Sculpture – in the form of a lion head – beckons at the end of a walkway. With his famous raised bed, Bill, 80, doesn't have to stoop down as much when he's planting and weeding. And the courtyard's brick paving means less lawn to mow, fewer weeds to pull and fewer leaves to rake. With its beautiful border, classical touches and practical appeal, Bill's courtyard garden makes a strong case for Mediterranean style in the Deep South.

ABOVE: By effectively massing a few old-fashioned flowers – foxglove, poppies, pinks and pansies – with a parsley edging, Bill gets the overgrown English look in late spring.

ABOVE: Travel to former French colonies in Polynesia opened Judy Green's eyes to the possibilities of a formal kitchen garden in Alabama.

Alabama Potager
Huntsville

PHOTOGRAPHY BY JENNIFER GREER AND CHARLOTTE HAGOOD

Anyone who has dreamed of having a classic kitchen garden in a suburban back yard will take heart from Judy Green in Huntsville. When she and her husband, Harold, moved to the suburbs, Judy set about transforming her hillside lot (once a limestone quarry) into her dream garden. Over the past several decades, she has created a series of gardens she calls Paradiso Verde. In 1994, with the help of her assistant, Susan Webb, Judy embarked on one of her most ambitious creations to date. The result is a formal garden reminiscent of a French potager with vegetables, herbs, fruit trees and flowers planted neatly in parterres, or geometric beds, defined by evergreen rosemary hedges. The four-square layout gives the illusion of European formality and brings order to food crops. Yet it's easily adapted to down-home Southern plants. Front and center is Judy's palatable selection of favorite vegetables, ranging from Kentucky Wonder green beans to Texas White Sweet onions. Classical ornaments, such as an armillary and a gargoyle fountain, provide a pleasing contrast to traditional country-garden fixtures, such as a muscadine arbor and bamboo bean towers. Old-fashioned sunflowers, marigolds and zinnias add color and character. Every square inch is planted with something pleasing to the palette – or the eye. For Judy, Paradiso Verde truly is a green paradise.

ABOVE: Formal design is best appreciated from above, and Judy's steep site allows her to enjoy the potager from her upper garden terrace. An evergreen rosemary hedge, boxwood, ornamental grasses and a pair of "Little Gem" magnolias define the long view.

OPPOSITE PAGE: Deep pink pentas, silvery artemisia and evergreen boxwoods encircle the armillary, which centers the four-square garden.

ABOVE: Classical touches such as a gargoyle fountain, create Old World charm.

Judy's Vegetable Picks

Pole Bean, Kentucky Wonder
Bush Bean, Italian Bunch
Beet, Detroit Red
Cantaloupe, Ambrosia
Carrot, Little Finger
Cowpea, Pink-Eye Purple Hull
Eggplant, Aubergine Black
    Enorma
Lettuce, Buttercrunch amd
    Sierra Romaine
Okra, Clemson Spineless
Onions, Texas White Sweet
Peppers, Golden Bell
Sweet Corn, Silver Queen
    and Ambrosia
Tomatoes, Beefsteak,
    Brandywine and Lillian's
    Yellow Heirloom
Watermelon, Sugar Baby

ABOVE: A circular stone pool, bordered by a cloud of artemisia, creates a mood of calm. Planted near the back wall, for protection from the cold, are Judy's favorite fruit trees.

TOP LEFT: "Sugar Baby" watermelon is a tasty space saver.

BOTTOM LEFT: "Teddy Bear" sunflowers are among Judy's favorites.

TOP RIGHT: "Summer Poinsettia," a re-seeding annual amaranth, makes a brilliant accent.

BOTTOM RIGHT: Judy grew "Millionaire," a hybrid Japanese eggplant, for summer stir-fry dishes.

Tropical Paradise
Anniston

PHOTOGRAPHY BY JENNIFER GREER AND CHARLOTTE HAGOOD

ABOVE: The show at Lost Palms peaks in late summer and early fall with a large collection of cannas.

Welcome to Lost Palms, a tropical paradise in Anniston, Ala., and, paradoxically, the foothills of the Appalachians. This may well be one of the most innovative – and loveliest – plant testing grounds in the South. "Plants don't read books. That's why my split-leaf philodendron is thriving outside in the ground along with other palms and tropicals," says Hayes Jackson, an energetic extension agent who grew up in Florida and was inspired by its tropical botany. Since 1992, he has created a series of botanical gardens atop a wooded ridge on the edge of town. Upon entering the back garden, guests stroll down a linear lawn past head-high ginger lilies (ripe with fragrance) and large, silky banana trees sporting exotic pink fruit. Hayes doesn't mind searching for the right microclimate – or wrapping a few prize palms in Christmas lights and blankets in January – to nourish something rare and wonderful. With mounting scientific evidence for global warming, Hayes just might be pioneering Alabama gardening for the 21st century.

ABOVE: Pink Velvet, a banana plant, is native to the Himalayas, but flourishes in Jackson's Anniston garden.

RIGHT: With a fondness for tropical plants and a master's degree in environmental biology and botany, Hayes Jackson has turned an Appalachian foothill into a gateway to the Caribbean.

OPPOSITE PAGE: A wide grass-covered path leads past a botanical perfume factory — ginger lilies — and other lush tropicals before ending in native pines.

ABOVE: Hayes' collection of ginger lilies, more than 50 varieties, reaches its height of bloom in September.

ABOVE: For Susan Lebold, cottage gardening is more than a style. It's a state of mind.

LEFT: Bonica (circa 1985)
was the first shrub rose to
be named an All-American
Rose Selection. It blooms
spring through fall in central Alabama.

ABOVE: Beautifully adapted to Alabama
gardens, New Dawn (circa 1930) is a fragrant, ever-blooming climber with, dark
green foliage.

RIGHT: Curving forms, masses of flowers
and horizontal lines give this small, English-
style garden a relaxed, feminine feel.

A Perfect Picture
Vestavia

PHOTOGRAPHY BY JENNIFER GREER AND CHARLOTTE HAGOOD

On a warm summer day, a baby smiles and coos for a photographer in Susan Lebold's Vestavia, back yard. Behind the child is Susan's baby — a picture-perfect flower garden that serves as a backdrop for friends' family portraits. At the end of Susan's suburban driveway, the modern world stops. An opening in a rusty wrought-iron fence, a classic garden bench and potted evergreens invite you to enter the small, but enchanting English-style cottage garden. Stepping stones curve through an emerald lawn accented with exuberant flower borders. Massed for effect are favorite Southern perennials — iris, coneflower, verbena, phlox, Queen Anne's lace, black-eyed Susan, coreopsis and Oriental lilies. Behind the perennials, flowering shrubs and vines, such as French hydrangea and sweet autumn clema-

ABOVE: Lebold lets an old rose ramble near the top of a fence, which gives it a strong background and creates a floating cloud of red blossoms.

tis, add structure and color. Spilling into paths and clambering over fences are new and old landscaping roses including New Dawn, Ballerina, Prosperity, Pink Perpetue, Bonica and Souvenir de la Malmaison. What's Susan's secret? "I'm a lazy gardener," she says. She smiles and

ABOVE: Introduced in 1937, Ballerina is a popular old rose for hedging. Prune it to shape or allow it to spill naturally over a fence.

explains that she uses only tried-and-true, easy-to-grow, Southern-strength plants. Lazy? Hardly. Smart? Indeed. No wonder friends want to capture family memories here. Stepping into Susan's garden is like stepping into a picture.

ABOVE: Hailing from 1919, Prosperity continues to win hearts with its sweet fragrance and large clusters of ivory flowers.

OPPOSITE PAGE: Stepping stones lead from the sunny front yard to a private courtyard that shelters bleeding heart, gardenias, tea olives and other cold-sensitive Southern favorites.

RIGHT: An 1870s Italianate cottage provides an ideal setting for Fennel Mauldin's reinterpretation of old styles.

Tennessee Valley Vernacular
Colbert County

PHOTOGRAPHY BY ED GIVHAN

When an artist comes to the garden, style undergoes reinvention, as in the case of Fennel Mauldin. Fennel developed a love of gardening from his mother and grandmother in a small farming community in the Tennessee Valley where he still lives. Today, he and his wife, Evelyn, share an imaginatively restored 19th century cottage with an equally creative landscape. The three-acre gardens feature a series of rooms and ever-changing canvases where Fennel works out his latest horticultural interests. These include collections of native plants, viburnum, hydrangea and David Austin English roses. Yet it's Fennel's whimsical reinterpretation of a traditional herb garden that first captures the eye. Classical references – an octagonal layout, a Hercules armillary and cut stone walls – contrast with light-hearted invention in the form of marble-studded pathways, bamboo tomato cages (topped with clay finials) and a voodoo-inspired bottle tree covered with yellow honeysuckle. If you ask Fennel about his success in the garden, he'll brag about his dirt. His lot was once wooded and is now covered with a foot of slightly acid, decayed leaf mold underpinned by the region's rich topsoil. "I grew up on a cotton farm and have been digging in the dirt all my life. It must be in my genes." This is a fun garden created in an original style best described as "folk formal" or, simply, pure Fennel Mauldin.

ABOVE: A handsome stone dry wall, classical circular step, potted plants and clumps of daylilies combine to announce a grand entrance to a side garden. Fennel salvaged the stones from the foundations and chimneys of old houses.

OPPOSITE PAGE: The color scheme for Fennel Mauldin's herb garden is fresh as a garden salad. It marries the cool greens of Egyptian onions, garlic chives, daylilies, parsley and thyme with the warm terra-cotta and mustard colors of the house and guesthouse. The octagonal design repeats the floor plan of the Italianate cottage.

ABOVE: A romantic cedar arbor covered with akebia vine and lit with a found light fixture marks a transition to the garden in the woods.

The Gifts of Herbs
Cullman

PHOTOGRAPHY BY JENNIFER GREER
AND CHARLOTTE HAGOOD

BELOW: Raised beds place fragrant herbs and flowers closer to eye level in a quiet seating area with Chippendale-style benches.

ABOVE: Silvery green cardoon hails from the Mediterranean and is at home with classical statuary in the herb garden.

ABOVE: Lavender, rosemary, cardoon and tansy weave a tapestry of textures studded with old-fashioned larkspur, a reseeding biennial.

OPPOSITE PAGE: A simple arbor, planted with the 1955 repeat-blooming climber, Dortmund, makes for a spectacular display in late spring with biennial foxglove.

There's a new trend called "smart gardening." It combines the use of well-adapted plants, common-sense techniques and low maintenance to beautiful effect. Only it's not new to Calera and Ronnie McHenry of CalMac Nursery in Cullman. The "test gardens" that she and her husband have created at their rural nursery attest to that. Behind the McHenrys' house and shop sit a series of terraced beds on a gently rolling slope. Curving lines and mounding plants give the landscape a natural feel. In late spring, both culinary and ornamental herbs – in varying shades of green, gray, yellow and blue – flourish in sunny, well-mulched islands. Traditional herb companions, such as larkspur, roses, foxglove, nasturtium and calendula, add splashes of blue, pink, yellow and orange. A few well-placed structures – an arbor, iron fence and Chippendale wooden benches – create focal points for plantings. Containers and statuary provide artful accents. A native of north Alabama, Calera grew up on a farm, where her mother grew herbs and taught her their many gifts. Today, she enjoys passing on her knowledge of herbs to other gardeners. "Herbs are flavorful, fragrant, beautiful and hardy. In the South, many of them are perennial. Others are annuals and biennials, and self-sow to return from seed every year. What other group of plants does all of those things?" Indeed, in Calera's garden, who could disagree?

RIGHT: Striking plant combinations – with tall, bronze, big-leafed cannas; clumps of melampodium; colorful pink pentas, and sprays of ornamental grass – give Ira's borders a sophisticated, yet natural look.

BELOW: Canna, Joe-pye weed, black-eyed Susan, sedum and salvia are signature plants of Ira's late summer beds.

English Country – in the City
Birmingham

PHOTOGRAPHY BY JENNIFER GREER
AND CHARLOTTE HAGOOD

ABOVE: Native black-eyed Susans and butterfly bush attract bees and butterflies to this country garden – in the heart of the city.

In 1975, when Ira Mitchell and his wife, Anne, bought a 1926, Federal-style house in Birmingham's historic Forest Park, the front yard was uninspiring. "It came with two hickory trees, a dogwood, yaupon holly and grass," he recalls, grimacing. Ira set out to rescue his new landscape. Soon, he was making trips to England to photograph country gardens and taking a course in landscape design at a nearby community college. Today, he operates his own garden-design service and enjoys a small, Southern-style English garden with an emphasis on formal structure and informal plantings. Ira set the tone for the garden by ringing the front walkway with a pleasing circle of lawn. In softly curving borders grows a progression of annual and perennial flowers, ornamental grasses and foliage plants, backed by a low, evergreen holly wall. The picture is completed by potted plants on the front terrace, with English ivy and other vines climbing up the side of the house. English-style borders call for a complex weaving of colors, textures and forms, plus a progression of blooms throughout the season. In spring, Ira relies on traditional cottage flowers, such as hollyhocks, foxglove, pinks and daisies for color. In summer, he fills the borders with Southern favorites, such as black-eyed Susan, Joe pye weed, sedum and salvia. "I'm trying to bring the country into the city," Ira confesses. And he's succeeding handsomely.

BELOW: A flower garden requires tending and watering on a regular basis, says Ira Mitchell. Hidden from the eye is a narrow path for weeding.

ABOVE: Potted plants help enclose the terrace; comfortable outdoor furniture creates an outdoor room for enjoying the garden and Forest Park neighbors.

Woods, Water and Wine

Lake Martin

PHOTOGRAPHY BY ED GIVHAN
AND JENNIFER GREER

"A garden design should be created like a rich novel … with an introduction, themes, surprises and twists of plots," says Jim Scott, a Montgomery attorney, hands-on gardener and master of the unexpected. For the past five years, he has been carving an Italian-inspired pleasure garden out of a wooded hillside at Lake Martin. This classical – and playful – landscape may be the last thing you expect to see within a few miles of boat launches and bait shops. Yet trust Jim to turn a summer afternoon into a virtual Roman holiday. He and his wife, Vivian, lead guests down a woodland path, past ancient boulders and a tumbling stream with multiple waterfalls – all man-made water features. Further along, tucked beneath a rock overhang, is an inviting grotto. As your eyes adjust to the low light, benches appear, along with shelves stocked with fine wines. The rush of waterfalls gives way to the happy sounds of a Mozart piano sonata, and you are temped to tarry. But wait, says Jim, grinning, there's more. He guides you up the hilly path, through a well-built Roman arch, to a giant chess game and a grand grassy court surrounded by a high stone wall with built-in benches. Up for a game of bocce? Once back to reality, on the Scotts' deck, you watch the sun set over Lake Martin, sip a glass of their fine wine – and can't wait to read Jim's next "novel."

ABOVE: Portals, such as this moon gate, lead from each garden room to the next, heightening a visitor's sense of anticipation.

ABOVE: Jim and Vivian Scott are avid gardeners. When they are not here enjoying their Lake Martin retreat, they are tending the lovely cottage garden at Grace Episcopal Church in Mt. Meigs.

OPPOSITE PAGE: Boulders were hauled in and painstakingly placed for effect in the Scotts' waterfall, which is set off by native trees, shrubs and ferns, and a surprise – a delicate cascade of impatiens.

INSET: A bust of Caesar is at home in a quiet corner with one of three chairs, each inscribed with a word from "Ecce quam bonum" Latin for "behold how good it is."

ABOVE: Jim's coliseum-style croquet/bocce court is also ideal for entertaining.

LEFT: "Chess anyone?" asks Jim as he prepares to play on a giant game board – and visual pun – with hand-carved wooden pieces.

OPPOSITE PAGE: Inside the grotto, the air feels refreshing at 60 degrees F.; looking outside, the arched doorway frames a view of rocks, water and forest, inviting contemplation.

Cathedral Woods
Mountain Brook

PHOTOGRAPHY BY CHARLOTTE HAGOOD

It's been said that a forest inspired the design of the gothic cathedral. Upon entering Weesie Smith's garden, it's easy to see why. Here, atop a wooded ridge near Shades Mountain, tall trees form a graceful, arching canopy, and sunlight streams through branches that become nature's stained-glass windows. In late March and early April, before the deciduous trees have fully leafed out, Alabama's woodland wildflowers awaken from winter's sleep. Nowhere is this event more joyful than on this four-acre property, where Weesie has spent more than 40 years grow-ing native plants. Just as spring moves northward day by day, it also moves upward through the forest. The first flowers emerge from the litter of leaves on the forest floor, followed by blooming vines, shrubs and trees, like a curtain slowly rising on a grand stage. This garden relies on mini-mal manmade structures, consisting mostly of a series of pathways, that open up the canopy so the understory plants can naturalize and bloom in broad sweeps. Certain plants, such as wild blue phlox, native Piedmont azalea and dogwood, weave throughout the garden and create a continuity of blue, pink and white against the emerging green. Up close, individual beauties, such as trillium, spi-derwort and atamasco lily, create a still life in an artist's gallery. Anyone who appreciates native plants will recog-nize that Weesie has carefully selected the most beautiful and garden-worthy species for spring. Indeed, this garden is the life's work of a dedicated plantswoman in step with the heartbeat of nature.

LEFT: Woodland paths open up the canopy to light, allowing plants, such as atamasco lily, blue phlox and ferns, to naturalize in Weesie Smith's native garden.

ABOVE: Atamasco lily is known as Alabama's native Easter lily.

ABOVE: Understory plants, such as the native Austrinum azalea, bloom in early spring before the tall hardwood trees com-pletely leaf out.

ABOVE: Spring-blooming natives – such as the pink Piedmont azalea, wild blue phlox and white dogwood – are concentrated along viewing areas.

RIGHT: Nature is unconcerned about shocking color combinations as evidenced by the simultaneuous bloom of the bright red fire pink and the wild blue phlox.

TOP: Wild hyacinth

ABOVE: Celandine poppy

TOP: Twisted trillium

ABOVE: Foam flower

TOP: American (northern) maidenhair fern

ABOVE: Spiderwort

BELOW: Exotic tropicals, such as geraniums, were favorites of late 19th century gardeners for use in containers in courtyard gardens.

BELOW: In Mobile's Church Street East Historic District, the Hamilton-Snider House was built in 1859 and restored by Virginia Snider's grandmother, Virginia Smith.

BELOW: A glassed-in gallery at the rear of the house allows the courtyard garden to be viewed from inside. Wonderfully mature tropical plants, such as a century-old date palm, a sago palm, large fatsia and split-leaf philodendron, are the legacy of Virginia's grandmother.

Oasis of History
Mobile

PHOTOGRAPHY BY ED GIVHAN

It's hard to believe that Ron and Virginia Snider's courtyard garden is across the street from the busy Spanish
Plaza, where Mardi Gras parades form in
downtown Mobile. Once you're behind these
elegant brick walls, it's like being in a natural
oasis. Water trickles like music from a cherubic
fountain. A flowering lemon tree perfumes the
air. Mature palms and other tropical plants
flourish in the sunny center, while ancient live
oaks tender shade on the street side. When
Virginia tells you the story of the garden, it
becomes an oasis of history as well. The 1859
Federal-style town home has roots in Mobile's
rich cultural past, with its lace grillwork on the
front porch and Spanish-influenced courtyard
in the rear. In 1969, Virginia's grandmother,
Virginia Smith, bought the house, restored it
and worked with a designer to create a courtyard garden in the traditional New Orleans
French Quarter style. Key elements include a
narrow, deep lot, brick paving and walls, raised
beds, a central fountain, ornate iron furniture, plus colorful blooming annuals, ferns, tender tropicals and citrus
trees (lemon and tangerine) planted in clay pots. Says
Virginia: "My grandmother was in her 70s when she created this garden. She had a much greener thumb than I
have, but I enjoy learning about the plants. This is a legacy
we want to preserve."

ABOVE: The New Orleans French Quarter
courtyard garden incorporates Spanish
influences, such as a central fountain.

RIGHT: Clair Matin, a French climbing rose, transforms a Chippendale-style arbor with symmetrical sprays of small, fragrant pink blooms.

BELOW: Claude Steele, a third-generation gardener, can enjoy a view of Mobile Bay from his garden.

BOTTOM: Claude's formal rose garden and boxwood parterres would have warmed the hearts of the French, who settled Mobile in 1702.

Bayside Charm
Battles Wharf

PHOTOGRAPHY BY ED GIVHAN

The strip of land along Mobile Bay at Battles Wharf includes a public footpath and affords one of the most spectacular strolls in Alabama. This is especially true when you pass Claude Steele's Victorian-style gardens, separated from the footpath with a waist-high, white picket fence. Even speed walkers slow down to admire the sprays of climbing roses that smother Claude's white Chippendale-style arbors. Finely edged boxwood parterres encircle prize specimens in the re-creation of a classic rose garden. A four-tiered fountain commands the center of this pictur-esque scene. Off to one side, a picket fence encloses neat rows of squash and other summer vegeta-bles. (Having been a retail grocer before retirement, Claude appreci-ates fresh vegetables.) Behind the rows, a conservatory-style green-house holds seedlings for the next season's garden. Claude learned to garden from his father when he was a child, and he fondly remem-bers helping his grandmother in her garden. Now he gardens for fun. For design, he draws on a mixture of Alabama influences from the Fairhope municipal rose garden and Bellingrath gardens to *Southern Living* maga-zine and local nurseries, which have also helped him build a collection of antique camellias. With roses from spring to fall, and camellias from fall to spring, Claude always has bouquets in the house for his wife.

TOP: Antique camellias are another of Claude's passions; he has more than 30 varieties.

ABOVE: The biggest problem in Claude's semitropical paradise is too much rain. As a result, all of Claude's beds are raised and French drains have been run under his gar-dens.

Moss Gallery
Florence

PHOTOGRAPHY BY JENNIFER GREER AND CHARLOTTE HAGOOD

Leave it to Maria Wall, an artist and relatively new gardener, to see something in the Alabama garden that most of us miss – the magic of moss. When Maria began gardening four or five years ago, she was caring for her mother at home and looking for a way to bring nature and beauty into their lives. A native of Italy, Maria loved sunny gardens and bright, colorful flowers. Yet her north Alabama lot was covered with shady woods and backed up into a boggy slough off the Tennessee River. Having worked as a fashion designer in New York, Maria saw the intrinsic beauty of the moss that grew in the woods. It carpeted the ground and draped the rocks and logs in folds of emerald green velvet. On a lark, she transplanted a few patches, watered the moss, and was delighted when it spread. Next, she found that annuals and perennials, such as impatiens, coleus, ferns, hosta, hardy begonia, and variegated ivy, added layers of color and texture to her moss garden.

ABOVE: Maria Wall possesses boundless energy and an artist's eye for originality, hence, her garden of folk-art sculpture and magical moss.

LEFT: Maria uses local materials, such as driftwood, rot-resistant cedar and stone, to create structures that invite you to explore and enjoy the garden.

Since then, Maria and her son, Frank, have blazed trails, revived streams, built small pools, moved stumps, and erected arches and arbors of driftwood (often given to her by her gardening friends) in the garden. At frequent intervals, visitors find rustic cedar shelters, benches and swings for rest and contemplation. It's no surprise that Maria's garden keeps growing. For her, a garden is an unfinished canvas. "I see an area, and I see what it could be," says Maria, her eyes bright with possibilities.

ABOVE: Maria reinterprets classical Roman arches into a rustic style befitting the Tennessee Valley.

TOP: True to her roots, this gardener loves classical statuary. At every twist and turn, she creates enchanting vignettes, such as a fawn resting on a velvet patchwork of moss.

ABOVE & RIGHT: Although working with a limited palette, Maria satisfies her thirst for color by massing shade-loving impatiens along a reconstructed stream. Against the backdrop of native woods, a simple but abundant mixture of impatiens, ferns and moss weave a garden tapestry.

BELOW: The lavender Catawba rhododendron grows wild along the banks of Little River; its blooming is a rite of spring in Mentone.

ABOVE: Native magnolias, such as the big-leaf variety, offer some of the most spectacular blooms in the forest.

Appalachian Spring
Mentone

PHOTOGRAPHY BY JENNIFER GREER
AND CHARLOTTE HAGOOD

On the banks of the West Fork of Little River, in the northeastern corner of Alabama, Ann and Bill Wright have a piece of Lookout Mountain. It could also be called a piece of heaven. The last frost arrives in early May, allowing the Wrights to grow many of the plants that thrive in the Smoky Mountains. By May, Appalachian spring comes to Menton, where the native oak-hickory-beech forest shelters mountain laurel, rhododendron and wild azaleas. In the Wrights' garden, mulch and grass paths follow the natural slope of the land, through dense and open woods, down to the river. There, the huge blossoms of the native Catawba rhododendron hang like paper lanterns over the water. Closer to the house, high shade provides a home for a variety of plant collections, including hostas, ferns, perennials and bulbs that thrive under the deciduous trees. In the fall, sugar maples infuse the garden with brilliant oranges. In the winter, Ann's collection of dwarf conifers, including weeping hemlock, adds welcome color and texture (even under a light dusting of snow). Mentone was settled as a cool escape from Birmingham's hot summers, yet this garden is pretty enough to escape to in any season.

BELOW: "Mountain laurel is considered by many to be our most beautiful shrub," wrote the late, great Alabama naturalist Blanche Dean.

ABOVE: Bill and Ann Wright make a good team. He likes big trees, shrubs and vines. She likes the shade-loving perennials that grow under them.

ABOVE: The native crossvine is found throughout Southern woodlands.

OPPOSITE PAGE: By May, spring comes to the hardwood forest on Lookout Mountain, and the shade garden responds to the warmer temperatures and dappled light.

RIGHT: The strategic placement of flower beds – within boxwood parterres and at the base of the fence – allows for a changing display of annuals, including the quintessential spring tulips, carefully timed to bloom with the crabapple.

BELOW: The upper gardens around the 1938 brick Georgian-style residence marry naturalistic and formal themes with a small boxwood parterre defined by a Belgian fence of native crabapple. At either end of the fence, is a free-form crabapple that connects the garden to the woodland behind it.

Stewardship and Style
Mountain Brook

PHOTOGRAPHY BY CHARLOTTE HAGOOD

Louise Wrinkle inherited a home set within a beautiful landscape created by her parents. The two-acre woodland is filled with mature native trees and shrubs, along with Japanese counterparts. A leading proponent of ecological and garden conservation, Louise has preserved the best of her parents' legacy. She also has employed a skilled hand and practiced eye to make the garden her own. In doing so, she has created a series of pocket gardens (garden rooms) near the house that engage the imagination and mark the seasons. During March, in a courtyard off the kitchen, you can best appreciate the sense of timing that a gardener like Louise has. The sunken Colonial-style garden features a clipped boxwood parterre with seasonal flower beds. It's defined by an elegant brick wall, which is pierced by a picket fence on three sides and is low-to-the ground in front to open the view. In front, a Belgian fence of blooming native crabapple casts a pink cloud over white tulips and pansies. This spring extravagance – resembling an Impressionist painting – is one of the joys Louise finds in her gardens and woodland.

ABOVE: Unmatched for its flowering show in early spring, crabapple is also deliciously fragrant. In the fall, the native Malus angustifolia sports red fruit the size of half-dollars.

Alabama, the Gardener's State

Alabamians have always been avid gardeners, as evidenced by historic gardens at Oakleigh in Mobile, Gaineswood in Demopolis, the Battle-Friedman House in Tuscaloosa, Pond Spring in Hillsboro and more. Today, however, we also benefit from a host of contemporary public gardens, which gardeners can visit for enjoyment and study. These gardens range from city squares to public parks, from botanical collections to arboreta, from corporate landscapes to historic hotels, and from state highway plantings to college campuses.

In this directory of more than 40 destinations, every effort has been made to capture the best gardens and landscapes in the state. Nevertheless, no doubt some have been missed, because gardens are constantly growing and changing. New travelers will seek out and find new gardens. As you travel, notice the eclectic mix of styles, because public gardens are seldom the vision of a single gardener. Professional designers, Master Gardeners, garden club members, nursery experts, teachers, horticulturists, volunteers and historic preservationists all have a hand in shaping them.

As you tour the state, expand your definition of a garden and take inspiration from a wildflower meadow, a farmer's hay sculptures, a historic cemetery, a country mailbox planting, or urban yard art. It would be cliché to say "stop and smell the roses." Yet in many ways, that's what gardening and garden travel are all about.

Each garden tells a unique story about Alabama and its landscape. Once you've hit the road, you'll see why Alabama can truly claim to be "the Gardener's State."

South Alabama Public Gardens

Bellingrath Gardens & Home

12401 Bellingrath Gardens Road
Theodore, AL 36582

What began in the 1920s as Bessie Morse Bellingrath's passion for collecting azaleas and camellias grew into one of the great country estate gardens of the South. (Bessie's husband, Walter, made a fortune in the Coca-Cola business.) When she ran out of planting space at her Mobile town house, she gardened at her husband's fishing camp on the Fowl River. After touring the great gardens of the world, the Bellingraths hired Harvard-trained architect George B. Rogers to help them design the 65 landscaped acres (amid the 905-acre wooded property), primarily in the English naturalistic style. Today, the garden features Mirror Lake, formal rose garden (2,500 bushes), conservatory (with an orchid collection), Great Lawn, bridal garden, chapel, Oriental-American garden, butterfly garden, rockery, new Ecological Bayou Boardwalk, river cruises and year-round floral displays. Under the new direction of William Barrick, formerly of Georgia's Callaway Gardens, perennial flower borders are being developed and the Oriental-American garden is being refurbished, among other improvements. Bellingrath is open daily

Bellingrath Gardens and Home

from 8 a.m. until one hour before sunset. Admission is $8.50 and up, depending on the tours taken. For information, call (251) 973-2217 or check out the Web site at www.bellingrath.org.

Biophilia Nature Center, Native Nursery and Bookstore

12695 County Road 95
Elberta, AL 36530

More than 300 species of native plants, some so ancient as to be prehistoric, thrive in this Baldwin County botanical restoration project. This combination garden/nursery/bookstore is one of the few places on earth where you can see the rare whisk fern, an ancient forest plant. The 20-acre Biophilia Nature Center educates with interpretive signs and nature herself in coniferous and mixed hardwood forests, a tupelo gum swamp, a pitcher plant bog and wildflower meadows. A butterfly house provides a nursery for showy butterflies and moths with eggs, caterpillars and chrysalises, in season. Everything from native beach plants to carnivorous pitcher plants and the Venus fly-trap can be seen here. Many unusual plants are for sale in the garden shop. Biophilia is usually open Tuesdays through Saturdays, 8 a.m. to 5 p.m., but it's a good idea to call ahead. Admission is $5, applied either to a tour or a purchase. For information, call (251) 987-1200 or check out the Web site at www.biophilia.net.

Conde-Charlotte Museum House
104 Theatre Street
Mobile, AL 36602
The Spanish ruled Mobile from 1780 to 1812, and to honor this legacy, an elegant replica of an 18th century walled Spanish garden has been built at the Conde-Charlotte Museum House. Adjacent to Fort Conde, the building was constructed in 1822-24 as the city's first jail and was converted to a Greek Revival town house two decades later. The National Society of Colonial Dames in Alabama built the garden in the 1950s, with its colonial four-square layout, boxwood parterres, evergreen plantings and central Spanish-tile fountain. The garden was researched and designed by Colonial Dame Ruth Bruckmann. It is open Tuesdays through Saturdays, from 10 a.m. to 4 p.m. Tours range from $2-$5. For information, phone (251) 432-4722 or check out the Web site at http://www.angelfire.com/al2/condechar-lotte/. NOTE: While in Mobile, you might enjoy a visit to the Richards-DAR House Museum in the heart of the De Tonti Square Historic District. The two-story, Italianate brick town house (circa 1860) includes a formal sitting garden, with evergreen trees, shrubs and parterres, as well as antique crape myrtles – more than 40 feet tall – as old as the house itself. For information, call (251) 208-7320.

Dothan Area Botanical Gardens
5130 Headland Avenue
Dothan, AL 36303
With development under way on the first 14 of 50 acres of land, the Dothan Area Botanical Gardens prides itself on being the only debt-free botanical garden in the United States. Enter through the wrought iron gates, get a brochure from the gardens' tent and enjoy a walking trail that loops through display areas. In spring and fall, more than 400 varieties of rose bushes grace the perimeter of the bricked garden. Wind past a raised herb garden and an allée of memorial oaks to plantings of daylilies, azaleas and camellias. Other niche gardens include a bog, a one-acre pond garden and a summer demonstration garden maintained by

Dothan Area Botanical Gardens

Master Gardeners, who donate the garden's fresh produce to the area's food bank. The gardens are adjacent to Landmark Park, an 1890s living history farm and Alabama's official Agricultural Museum. Dothan's garden is open seven days a week. Admission is free. For more information, call (334) 793-3224 or check out the Web site at www.dabg.com.

Eufaula's Fendall Hall and Pilgrimage
917 West Barbour Street
Eufaula, AL 36027
This handsome antebellum Italianate mansion (circa 1860) was passed down through four generation of Young family women, all of whom apparently loved gardening. Old-fash-

ioned flowering shrubs from antebellum and Victorian periods cloak the house. They include familiar Southern favorites, such as spirea, boxwood, ligustrum, roses, azaleas, oleander, pittosporum, banana shrub and camellias. Upon entering the garden, visitors pass a three-tiered fountain, installed in the 1880s. (Fendall Hall was the first home in town to have running water, and the fountain reportedly shot water 20 feet in the air!) Today, the Alabama Historical Commission operates Fendall Hall. Inside the house, a collection of hand-painted murals (dating from 1884) is based on romantic motifs, including hollyhocks, roses and lilies the artist plucked from the garden. The best time to see Fendall Hall, along with the rest of the historic homes in Eufaula, is on the first weekend in April when the town has its famous pilgrimage. Fendall Hall is open Mondays through Saturdays from 10 a.m. to 4 p.m. Admission is $4. For information, call (334) 687-8469 or check out www.eufaulapilgrimage.com

Fairhope Municipal Rose Garden

1 Fairhope Avenue
Fairhope, AL 36532
Looking up from the rows of roses and boxwoods, visitors to the Fairhope Municipal Rose Garden are rewarded with a spectacular view of Mobile Bay. Rich red and vivid pink roses against water and sky craft a painterly picture at the Fairhope Municipal Pier. More than 800 roses bloom from April to November in this formal French-style garden with an ornate, tiered fountain and clipped boxwood parterres. Started by a single citizen who loved roses, the garden is now a city project and the subject of community pride. The roses generally peak in May around Mother's Day, but bloom off and on for at least eight months. The garden includes an All-America Rose bed, which the city staff monitor for successful new varieties for the Deep South. Fairhope has a city horticulturist, and the public plantings throughout the city are worth seeing. The rose garden is open daily. Admission is free. For more information, call (251) 928-2136 or check out the Web site at www.cofairhope.com/tourism.html.

Gaineswood

805 South Cedar Avenue
Demopolis, AL 36732
Gaineswood has been described as "one of the three or four most interesting houses in America" by "The Smithsonian Guide to Historic America: Deep South." Demopolis cotton planter Nathan Bryan Whitfield was the innovative owner-architect behind the antebellum Greek Revival mansion. He distinguished the house with its domed architecture, elaborate ceilings, marble mantles, wood graining and fine plasterwork, among other features. Outside, the grounds were equally impressive. Even today, extensive lawns and a crape myrtle allée raise expectations when visitors approach the mansion, perched Parthenon-style atop a hill. In the front and back of the house, two formal balustraded gar-

Fairhope Municipal Rose Garden

dens extend like a grand stage. Antebellum features include boxwood parterres, classical statuary, wrought-iron urns, benches and gates. In front, a statue of Pomona, Roman goddess of fruit, commands attention. Old-fashioned shrubs fill the gardens and dot the landscape. In the distance sits a small, domed neo-classical style temple, which Whitfield called his summerhouse and music pavilion. Thanks to an 1860 engraving, historians have an accurate vision of the planter's "folly landscape," one designed to amuse its owner as much as the guests. A National Historic Landmark, Gaineswood recently underwent restoration, says Historic Site Director Matthew Hartzell, who is working with site staff to enhance the gardens with period and heirloom bulbs – white narcissus, daffodil and snowdrops. Gaineswood is open daily and Sundays, and is closed on major holidays. Tours are held on the hour, yet the hours are seasonal. Admission is $5 for adults, $3 for children ages 13-18 and $2 for children 6-12. For information, phone (334) 289-4846 or check out the Web site at www.preserveala.org.

Minamac Wildflower Bog & Country Gardens

13199 MacCartee Lane
Silverhill, AL 36576
Anyone who has ever visited the Minamac Wildflower Bog & Country Gardens in Silverhill, five miles east of Fairhope, understands what a magical place this is. And why these gardens have been featured in "Southern Living" and on national television. With a five-acre lake and walking paths, these privately owned gardens have preserved some of the most unusual wild plants in the state, including lower Coastal Plain pitcher plants. Fields

Minimac Wildflower Bog

of these trumpet-shaped carnivorous plants stand at attention. Other uncommon beauties appear in the bog, including the native fringed orchid, southern pine lily, blazing star and goldencrest. In all, more than 300 varieties of native plants are featured with their blooms painting and re-painting the landscape in bright reds, magentas, purples and yellows from spring through fall. A two-acre, old-fashioned garden spotlights traditional Southern plantings. Garden rooms open to spectacular views of wildflower meadows. Minamac is open April through September with tours by reservation only. Admission charges vary. For information, call (251) 945-6157 or check out the Web site at www.auburn.edu/awac/places/minimac.htm.

Mobile Botanical Gardens

5151 Museum Drive
Mobile, AL 36608
A fabulous herb garden, peaceful nature trails, outstanding collections of rhododendrons and native azaleas, a classic camellia garden and a stately holly garden are among the highlights of the Mobile Botanical Gardens. In this historic city, these community gardens were established in 1974 by a dedicated group of Mobile horticulturists to preserve the natural habitat of the Gulf Coast. Today, the gardens include more than 100 acres of natural woodlands, including remnants of the great Southern longleaf pine forest as well as cultivated gardens and open spaces. Magnolia,

Mobile Botanical Gardens

holly, azalea, rhododendron and camellia gardens reflect the pioneering work of Mobile-area nursery owners in breeding these trees and shrubs. A fragrance and texture garden is designed to make the sensory delights of the garden accessible to disabled visitors. A fern glade and small swamp flourish in the wetter areas. With an active educational program, the Mobile Botanical Gardens are fast becoming a cultural center for plant lovers in the region. The gardens are open from 8 a.m. to 5 p.m. daily. Admission is $2 for children and $4 for adults. For information, phone (251) 342-0555.

Oakleigh

350 Oakleigh Place
Mobile, AL 36604
Mobile's official period house museum, Oakleigh was built atop a hill in a grove of live oaks, some of which are more than 300 years old. Once a country retreat, it is now part of the city's Oakleigh Garden District. The small, circa-1833 Greek Revival temple looks out over 3.5 acres of shady lawns, live oaks, magnolias, camellias and azaleas. Among the more interesting landscape features is a circa-1920 sunken garden, which was installed by a land-scape architect for the Cole family. The sunken garden measures 200 feet by 65 feet, with embankments 20 feet high. Formal columns and urns mark the entry to this garden, with steps descending into an emerald green lawn, a circular pool and a tiered, wrought-iron fountain. Oakleigh is on the National Register of Historic Places and is the home of the Historic Mobile Preservation Society. The society recently obtained a grant to restore the antebellum landscape and sunken garden. It also plans to add two 19th century-style kitchen gardens, including one at the nearby Cox-Deasy House, an 1850s raised Creole cottage. The museum is open Mondays through Saturdays, from 10 a.m. to 4 p.m., and is closed on holidays. Admission is $5 for adults and $4 for children 6-12. For information, call (251) 432-1281 or check out the Web site at www.historicmobile.org.

St. James Hotel

1200 Water Avenue
Selma, AL 36701
Built in 1837, the elegant St. James Hotel in Selma gave the stamp of refinement to the 19th century Alabama Riverfront. It had been converted to a tire recapping plant, when city planner Elizabeth Driggers pushed for its restoration in the mid 1990s. Today, thanks to a community-wide effort, the St. James is one of the few remaining riverfront antebellum hotels in the United States. It boasts stylish interiors – with 19th century colors, period antiques and 1850s French silk draperies. The hotel also includes a classic New Orleans-style courtyard garden, reflecting Alabama's Spanish and French influences. Designed by local preservation architect Richard Hudgens, the courtyard garden features a brick plaza, central

fountain and ornate urns full of potted plants and large tropical palms. The hotel restaurant, the Troup House, looks out onto the garden. If you plan your visit in March, you might catch Selma's famous pilgrimage, home tour and antique show. For information, call (334) 872-3234 or see the Web site at www.selmaalabama.com.

Sturdivant Hall

713 Mabry Street

Sturdivant Hall

Selma, AL 36701 Imposing white columns and black iron lace embellish the facade of Sturdivant Hall, a Selma town house that's been called "the finest Greek Revival Neo-Classic Antebellum Mansion in the Southeast." Follow the boxwood-edged, herringbone brick path into the stately mansion (circa 1852), and you'll see why it is on the National Register of Historic Places. In addition to the fine architecture, paintings and antiques, the house boasts a replica 19th century strolling garden outside its rear door. The French-style garden dates back to the 1950s, when Natchez, Miss., architect Earl Hart Miller was called in to restore Sturdivant Hall. Formal brick paths, evergreen plantings and an ivy-covered brick wall define a long central lawn. Nearer the house, a smaller parterre-shaped lawn surrounds a circular, tiered fountain that glistens in the sunlight. Pocket gardens include old-fashioned plants, such as coral vine, mock lemon, tea olive and culinary herbs. The house museum is open Tuesdays

Fair Oaks Square

through Saturdays from 10 a.m. to 4 p.m. Admission is $5 for adults and $2 for students. For information, phone (334) 872-5626 or check out the Web site at www.selmaalabama.com. NOTE: Only a block away from Sturdivant Hall is Fair Oaks Square in Selma's Old Town. This restored city block offers an excellent walking tour of turn-of-the-century cottages and gardens.

Troy State University Arboretum

Troy State University
Troy, AL 36082
Alabama's Wiregrass region is home to an unusual plant community that is being preserved and studied at the Troy State University Arboretum. The arboretum includes 75 acres adjacent to the main campus and an 18-acre Pocosin Preserve, six miles east of the main campus. It also maintains nature trails and serves as a site for picnics and bird-watching. The arboretum is open from sunrise until sunset, seven days a week. Guided tours and programs may be arranged. For information, call (334) 670-0848 or check out the Web site at www.troyst.edu/pubserv/html/pub6.html.

Central Alabama Public Gardens

Advent Gardens

2017 6th Avenue North
Birmingham, AL 35203
Opened in 1959, the Advent Gardens are located in the courtyard of the Cathedral Church of the Advent. On 20th Street in downtown Birmingham, visitors can find solitude under the canopy of a tall oak in the Rectors Garden. Elegant and symbolic, this is a "white garden" (green background plantings with white pansies, tulips, narcissus, variegated ivy, azaleas and hydrangeas). It also includes classical fountains and statuary. On the north side of the church, in the Betty Turner Garden, Japanese maples form an allée that is underplanted with shade-loving perennials, such as Lenten rose, Solomon's seal, hostas and ferns. Around the corner is a delightful nook with a wishing well. The church's St. Fiacre Guild helps plant and maintain the Advent Gardens, which are open daily, from 8 a.m. to 5 p.m., and on Sundays, from 8 a.m. to 1 p.m. For information, call (205) 251-2324.

Aldridge Gardens

Lorna Road and Rocky Ridge Ranch Road
P.O. Box 360246
Hoover, AL 35236
When completed, the 30-acre Aldridge Gardens will contain the world's largest hydrangea collection – French, Snowhill, Snowflake, Annabelle, Peegee, oakleaf, climbing, etc. – with a flowering display from spring through fall. The gardens and woodlands were once the private estate of Birmingham nurs-

Oakleaf hydrangea, Aldridge Gardens

eryman Eddie Aldridge and his wife, Kay. The Aldridges are working in collaboration with the city of Hoover to open the grounds to the public. The property includes a seven-acre lake, residence (future Visitor's Center) and a series of pocket gardens and trails through the woods. A master plan calls for transforming the site into a showcase for woodland plants, plus a butterfly garden, children's garden, fragrance garden and waterfall garden. Aldridge Gardens are scheduled to open in late spring 2002. For information, call the city at (205) 682-8019 or check out the Web site at www.hooveral.org/content/development/aldridgegardens.

American Village

State Highway 119
P.O. Box 6
Montevallo, AL 35115
Located at the American Village in Montevallo, the Southern Living Colonial-style garden offers a convenient way to travel back to the days of George and Martha Washington. Their historic Virginia farm, Mount Vernon, inspired this new 113-acre civic-education facility. Although American Village is designed to be a hands-on educa-

tional experience for children, adult visitors can stroll through the gardens just behind Washington Hall. The hall overlooks an 18th-century style pleasure garden based on a traditional four-square design with evergreen parterres, small accent trees, seasonal floral displays and a white picket-fence border. (The staff of *Southern Living* magazine designed and now maintain the garden.) The American Village is open Mondays through Fridays, from 10 a.m. to 4 p.m. Admission is $9 for adults, $8 for seniors and $6 for students. For information, call (205) 665-3535 or check out the Web site at www.americanvillage.org.

Arlington Antebellum Home & Gardens

331 Cotton Avenue
Birmingham, AL 35211
The historic Arlington Antebellum Home & Gardens are located on six acres in the heart of Elyton, the first permanent county seat of Jefferson County. A fine example of Greek Revival architecture from the 1840s, the house was built by Judge William S. Mudd, a Birmingham founder. The home is furnished with a collection of 19th century decorative arts, and the surrounding gardens reflect both antebellum and Edwardian influences. These include Victorian-style flowerbeds, kitchen/cutting garden, charming water garden and century-old boxwood allée (a favorite of local brides), plus several handsome willow oaks and other large trees true to the antebellum period. Hours are Tuesdays through Saturdays, from 10 a.m. to 4 p.m., and Sundays, from 1 p.m. to 4 p.m. Visitors can stroll the gardens free of charge. Admission to the house is $5 per adult and $3 per student 6 to 18 years old. Arlington is closed on Mondays and city holidays. For information, call (205) 780-5656 or check out the Web site at www.al.us/arlington/default.jspci.bham.

Battle-Friedman House

1010 Greensboro Avenue
Tuscaloosa, AL 35401

Gazebo, Battle-Friedman House

What may be the oldest intact antebellum garden in the state surrounds the Battle-Friedman House on Greensboro Avenue in Tuscaloosa. This brick Classical Revival townhouse was built in the 1830s, yet it's believed that the landscape was the main attraction. In 1847, the Battle family commissioned an English garden designer to design a formal strolling garden – with intersecting brick paths and diamond-shaped beds – that occupied an entire city block. In 1875, the Battles sold the house to the Friedman family, who added Victorian touches, such as the gazebo. Today, the Tuscaloosa County Preservation Society maintains the house and surrounding gardens. In 1997, through a donation from Anne Boyd Russell, the gardens under went restoration under the direction of Birmingham landscape architect Jane Reed Ross. The house and garden are open Tuesdays through Saturdays, from 10 a.m. to noon and 1 p.m. to 4 p.m., and Sundays, from 1 p.m. to 4 p.m. Visitors can stroll the gardens free of charge. The cost to see the house is $3. For information, call (205) 758-6138 or check out the Web site www.historictuscaloosa.org.

Birmingham Botanical Gardens

Birmingham Botanical Gardens

2612 Lane Park Road
Birmingham, AL 35223
From the most formal to the most natural, these 67.5 acres are home to more than 25 display gardens, including those showcasing popular Southern plants: roses, irises, daylilies, camellias, herbs, vegetables, rhododendrons, ferns and wildflowers. Opened in 1962, the Birmingham Botanical Gardens were designed by the celebrated 20th-century landscape architect Robert Marvin. They represent the largest municipally owned botanical gardens in the Southeast. At one end of the property, visitors can find a quiet place for meditation in the Japanese Gardens, one of the finest of its kind in the country. At the opposite end, the Kaul Wildflower Garden takes visitors up an Appalachian foothill covered with a superb collection of native plants. In between sit two rose gardens (one modern and one old-fashioned), a Southern Living Garden and the Conservatory, the largest clearspan greenhouse in the region. The outdoor sculpture and architectural features (including an authentic Japanese teahouse) throughout the gardens, as well as the horticultural library and gift shop

at the Garden Center, are outstanding. The Birmingham Botanical Gardens are open year-round, from dawn to dusk. Admission is free. For information, call (205) 414-3950 or check out the Web site at www.bbgardens.org.

Blount Cultural Park/ Shakespeare Garden

6055 Vaughn Road
Montgomery, AL 36116
As a Montgomery high-school English teacher, Carolyn Blount brought a passion to teaching of the works of William Shakespeare. The desire of Carolyn and her husband, Wynton M. "Red" Blount to leave a legacy to the people of Alabama resulted in which opened the 300-acre Blount, Cultural Park in the mid 1980s. The center of the park is the Carolyn Blount Theatre, which houses the nationally known Alabama Shakespeare Festival. With the goal of creating an English-style landscape park as a setting for the theater, the Blounts hired pre-imminent English landscape architect Russell Page of London. With its wood-and-stone bridges, groves of trees, Elizabethan-styled structures and quaint lakes – dotted with black and white swans – the park succeeds in transporting visitors to 16th century England. In 2000, the Shakespeare Garden and Amphitheatre were completed. This replica of an Elizabethan garden – complete with wattle fencing, twig arbors, leafy bowers, thatched-roof huts and many plants mentioned in the bard's plays – was designed by Edwina von Gal & Co. of New York. The park and garden are open year-round, from 9 a.m. to 9 p.m. Admission is free. For information, call (334) 274-0062 or check out the Web site at www.blountculturalpark.org.

Charles W. Ireland Sculpture Garden

Birmingham Museum of Art
2000 8th Avenue North
Birmingham, AL 35203

The Birmingham Museum of Art takes the traditional courtyard concept and uses it as a starting point for a modern oasis of art in the Charles W. Ireland Sculpture Garden. Upon entering the garden, visitors find a shady harbor on iron benches in a plaza beneath towering water oaks. The leafy canopy is underplanted with lush ferns, hostas, other shade-loving perennials, evergreen shrubs and small trees. The benches overlook the Blue Pools Courtyard, which reflects azure colors all the way to the top of the museum's striking 2 1/2 story bow window. The courtyard is one of three outdoor rooms where visitors can enjoy the works of Rodin, Botero and other internationally known sculptors. Other areas include a sunken garden for temporary shows and a raised plaza for permanent exhibits, including a granite waterfall by sculptor Elyn Zimmerman. The largest outdoor space for viewing art in the Southeast, the garden was designed by Zimmerman in collaboration with lead architect Edward Larrabee Barnes. The sculpture garden is open Tuesdays through Saturdays, from 10 a.m. to 5 p.m., and Sundays, from noon to 5 p.m. It is closed Mondays and holidays. Admission is free. For information, call (205) 254-2565 or check out the Web site at www.artsBMA.org.

Donald E. Davis Arboretum, Auburn University

101 Rouse LSB
Auburn University, AL 36849

Many a student has learned to identify Alabama trees in the Donald E. Davis Arboretum on the edge of campus at Auburn University. Anyone interested in horticulture, forestry, botany or ecology would enjoy the 14-acre teaching garden. It's home to nearly 200 species of trees, including some large, 100-year old-post oaks and loblolly pines. The botanical collection includes native climbers, shrubs and other understory plants. The arboretum was established in 1963 and was named after a retired ecology professor who led the way for its creation. It's open daily from sunrise to sunset. Admission is free. For information, call (334) 844-5770 or check out the Web site at www.auburn.edu/academic/science_math/arboretum. **NOTE:** While here visit the Garden of Memory in honor of American veterans.

EcoScape

Birmingham-Southern College
Birmingham, AL 35254

Built atop a dump, this environmentally friendly garden demonstrates the rehabilitation possible with almost any landscape. EcoScape opened in 1996 as the outdoor classroom for the Southern Environmental Center at the Birmingham-Southern College. Designed by Alexander Vare, the garden invites young visitors to explore the ancient workings of a sundi-

Sculpture garden, Birmingham Museum of Art

al, meander past rock-slab walls, and marvel at giant insect sculptures (original art enhances learning throughout the garden). Children pause in a raised circular garden (with concentric beds) to sample edible and aromatic plants. They watch the dance of butterflies in a flower border carefully planted to attract the winged creatures. Children also discover natural Alabama along the Native Plant Walk, which features three ecosystems – woodland, sunny meadow and forest edge – in a short hike. With its conservation focus, EcoScape provides an ideal setting for teaching people about organic gardening as well as water issues ranging from Xeriscaping to non-point source pollution. EcoScape is open daily from dawn to dusk. Admission is free. For information call (205) 226-4770 or check out the Web site at www.bsc.edu/sec/ecoscape.

Flower Hill, University of Montevallo

University of Montevallo
Montevallo, AL 35115

Famous for its red brick streets and paths, the University of Montevallo campus should also be known for its connection with the Olmsted Brothers. This landscape architecture firm was founded by Frederick Law Olmsted, the creator of New York's Central Park. In the 1920s, the university hired the Brookline, Mass., firm (then headed by Olmsted's brother and son) to develop the first plan for the historic 160-acre campus. The plan worked with the natural landscape, the travel patterns of students and existing historic structures, including two antebellum buildings in the central National Historic District. Today, sweeping lawns, groves of trees and flowerbeds enhance the 40 buildings around the campus. Thanks to people such as David Pritchett, who oversees the

Flower Hill, University of Montevallo

grounds, the Olmsted Brothers' basic design ideas are still followed. One of the places this can be seen is at Flower Hill, the circa-1926 residence of the university's president. A herringbone brick road runs through an allée of pecan trees up to the Georgian mansion. Rebecca Fuller Harmon, wife of the first president to occupy the house, planted flower borders around the mansion and maintained them throughout her 20-year stay.

These borders prompted townspeople to name the house Flower Hill. The campus is open year-round. Admission is free. For more information, call (205) 665-6230 or check out the Web site at www.montevallo.edu/admissions/tour.

Grace Episcopal Church

100 Old Pike Road
P.O. Box 24
Mt. Meigs, AL 36057

The Carpenter Gothic-style church was popular in central Alabama in the latter half of the 19th century. In Mt. Meigs, Ala., 10 miles east of Montgomery, garden travelers can find a classic example at Grace Episcopal Church. The church has survived with few alterations since its construction in the 1890s and has an active congregation. About 20 years ago, Jim and Vivian Scott of Montgomery, both talented gardeners, took the churchyard under their wing. They surrounded it with a series of gardens, each serving some aspect of church life. The front beds are planted in English cottage-garden style, brimming with old fashioned Southern flowers: larkspur, rose campion, opium poppies, ragged robin, sweet William and phlox. To the north of the church sits a lovely graveyard. It's bordered on the west side by a 100-foot English-style flower border, supplying cut flowers for the altar. Nearby grows a rose garden with more than 60 bushes, including old-fashioned varieties. In the rear of the church, brick walls enclose a patio enveloped by a lushly planted shade garden (full of ferns, hosta, fatsia and other foliage plants and shrubs). Grace Church's gardens are open year-round. For information, call (334) 215-1422.

Helen Keller
Fragrance Garden for the Blind

Alabama Institute for the Deaf and Blind
205 East South Street
P.O. Box 698
Talladega, AL 35161

For Helen Keller, one of Alabama's most famous garden enthusiasts, fragrance was an important part of childhood memory. In her autobiography, she recalls wandering outdoors at the age of seven and suddenly smelling an incredibly sweet fragrance. She followed her nose to the blossoms of a mimosa tree, and climbed up into it. "I sat there for a long time, feeling like a fairy on a rose cloud," she wrote. In Talladega, home to the Alabama Institute for the Deaf and Blind, the members of the Garden Club of Alabama were fascinated by Helen's descriptions of strolling in a garden

and soaking up the different scents. In 1961, they developed a plan for a fragrance garden to be enjoyed by the students and staff at the Alabama School for the Blind. Smooth walkways and handrails make navigating easy. Raised beds put fragrant plants – herbs, bulbs, perennials and shrubs – at nose level. Open year-round from dawn to dusk, the garden is set in the institute's century-old campus in Talladega's Historic District. Admission is free. For information, call (256) 761-3259. For information on the city's spring pilgrimage, see the Web site at www.talladegawalk.com.

Japanese Garden,
Gulf States Paper Corporation

1400 Jack Warner Parkway
Tuscaloosa, AL 35404

A small island, such as Japan, must think big: the rock is a mountain, the pool is the ocean, the bonsai tree is a forest. Designed by David Engel, the Japanese Garden at the corporate headquarters of Gulf States Paper in Tuscaloosa exemplifies this philosophy. Only full-length glass windows separate the offices from the serene garden, which is located in the center of the corporate buildings. The most striking feature, a one-acre pond, is home to

Japanese Garden, Gulf States Paper Corporation

koi, exotic black-necked geese and mallards. Japanese architecture, statuary and brilliant peacocks add to the exotic feeling, painting a picture of harmony within controlled nature. A two-acre Alabama woodland surrounds the buildings, reminding visitors of the greater natural world. Inside the headquarters building, visitors can enjoy the Warner Collection, one of the most extensive private collections of fine American art. The garden and art gallery are testimony to the cultural vision of Jack Warner, the company's former chief executive officer. The Japanese Garden is open during business hours year-round. Free tours are offered Saturdays and Sundays, from, 1 p.m. to 4 p.m. For information, call (205) 562-5000.

Jasmine Hill Gardens and Outdoor Museum

3001 Jasmine Hill Road
Montgomery, AL 36093
The marble beauty of Venus de Milo glows against the backdrop of blooming cherry trees. "Winged Victory" watches over a child playing in the reeds by a reflecting pool. A bust of Socrates wisely welcomes visitors down an allée of flowering azaleas, dogwoods and magnolias. Where else but Jasmine Hill Gardens and Outdoor Museum can you find the cultural legacy of ancient Greece in a garden with Renaissance elegance set against a backdrop of beloved Southern plants? From the 1920s to the 1960s, founders Benjamin and Mary Fitzpatrick visited Greece and brought back more than 40 recreations of classical statuary and architecture, including a replica of the ruins of the Temple of Hera. Today, another dedicated couple, Jim and Elmore Inscoe of Montgomery oversee the garden, which operates as a non-profit organization for the enjoyment and education of the public. Jasmine Hill covers 20 acres atop a wooded knoll and includes a handsome, new visitor center (in Greek-temple style designed by Montgomery architect Jim Barganier). A lighting system enhances full moon strolls and other special evening events. The garden puts on a flowering show year-round, but the blooming of the cherry trees in late March and early April is a rite of spring for many visitors. In the summer, crepe myrtles, including the largest in the state, paint the garden with color. Jasmine Hill is open Tuesdays through Sundays, from 9 a.m. to 5 p.m., and is closed holidays. Admission is $5 for adults, $3 for children 6-12 and free for children under 6. For information, call (334) 567-6463 or check out the Web site at www.jasminehill.org.

Old Alabama Town

301 Columbus Street
Montgomery AL 36104
Old Alabama Town in Montgomery is a time machine propelling visitors backward 150 or more years. Buildings and other artifacts from central Alabama have been brought together to re-create a 19th century pioneer village. The

Old Alabama Town

surrounding yards and gardens are as interesting as the historic structures. They include a village green, scuppernong grape arbor, swept yards, spring cutting gardens and an herb garden at the corner of Hull and Columbus streets. Heirloom herbal formulas made the lives of Alabama pioneers more pleasant and healthful, as visitors learn on the Living Block Tour – which includes the herb garden. Beds brim with oregano, rosemary, germander, thyme, lemon grass, garlic and various other fragrant, savory and medicinal herbs. Old Alabama Town is open Mondays through Saturdays, from 9 a.m. to 3 p.m. Admission is $7 for adults and $3 for students. For information, call (334) 240-4500 or check out the Web site at www.oldalabamatown.com.

Petals from the Past

16034 County Road 29
Jemison, AL 35085
There's no better place to appreciate heirloom plants than at Petals from the Past in Jemison, about a mile from I-65. Here, garden travelers learn something their grandmothers knew all along. Old-fashioned plants appeal to the senses, are hardy performers and stir memories. More than a garden shop and nursery, Petals features a 1930s-era farmhouse and a traditional, four-square pleasure garden for displaying vintage plant treasures. Quaint arbors support flowering vines and climbing roses. Fences brace tall seed-grown annuals, such as larkspur, cleome and zinnia. Neat beds overflow with herbs, polyantha roses, bulbs and perennials. Owner Jason Powell and his wife, Shelley, opened the shop in 1994. Petals from the Past is open Tuesdays through Saturdays, from 9 a.m. to 5 p.m., and Sundays, from 1 p.m. to 5 p.m. For information, call (205) 646-0069.

Petals from the Past

Prattvillage Gardens

Heritage Center
102 East Main Street
Prattville, AL 36067,
Among the surprises at Old Prattvillage in Prattville is a weathered, Gothic-style chapel (see photo page 97) resting in the middle of a cottage garden maintained by the Master Gardeners of Autauga County. A picket fence encloses an herb garden, a billowy butterfly and hummingbird walk and a perennial sampler garden. Old-fashioned flowers, such as zinnias, cosmos, purple coneflower and black-eyed Susan, grow with abandon. Vine-covered arbors and vintage shrubs add to the nostalgia of the setting. The gardens are open daily. Admission is free. For information, phone (334) 361-0961 or check out the web site at www.prattville.com/visitor/history.

University of Alabama Arboretum

P.O. Box 870344
Tuscaloosa, AL 35487-0344
As wild gardens go, the 60-acre University of Alabama Arboretum is already a gem, and it promises to become one of the state's showcases for native- plant ecosystems. Sponsored by the university's Department of Biology, this

UA Arboretum

outdoor classroom was founded in 1958 and features walking trails through mature woods (trees are labeled by species). Among the more innovative aspects is the canopy walk, one of only a few in the South. This platform puts school children 40 feet up in the air – eye to eye with canopy creatures – to study "Tree Topology." Under the direction of horticulturist Mary Jo Modica, the arboretum has begun developing a new master plan with Darrel G. Morrison, one of the nation's leading architects of ecological landscapes. The arboretum is open daily, from 8 a.m. to 5 p.m. Admission is free. For information or to order a plant-sale catalog, call (205) 553-3278 or check out the Web site at www.bama.ua.edu/~arbor.

William Bartram Arboretum

Fort Toulouse Jackson Park
2151 West Fort Toulouse Road
Wetumpka, AL 36093
"This is perhaps one of the most eligible situations for a city in the world, a level plain between the conflux of two majestic rivers..." More than 200 years ago, the great naturalist and frontier explorer William Bartram traveled to Fort Toulouse, north of where two great rivers – the Coosa and the Tallapoosa – converge. In his historic book, *Travels of William Bartram*, he described the native plants and animals he found here and throughout Alabama and the Deep South. Today, an arboretum is dedicated to his achievement. Begun in cooperation with the Garden Club of

America, the arboretum includes a walkway designed for elderly and disabled visitors. The trails curve past wildflower meadows, wetlands and woodland habitats towards a river overlook. The arboretum is open year-round. Hours are from sunup to sundown. Admission to the park is $2 for adults and $1 for students. For information, call (334) 567-3002 or check out the Web site at www.wetumpka.al.us/features.html.

Wildflower/Restless Natives

234 Oak Tree Trail
Wilsonville, AL. 35186
In 1994, when Jan Midgley and Dean Clark opened their business, it was one of central Alabama's first nurseries and outlets devoted to Southeastern natives. Jan specializes in growing native wildflowers, ferns and herbaceous plants. Dean brokers native trees and shrubs for gardeners doing major landscaping projects. The couple is developing a series of study gardens – a sunny meadow, a wet meadow, and two woodland gardens, one seasonally moist and one dry, around their house on their five-acre property. In 1999, Jan pulled together 30 years of experience in growing native plants when she published a series of excellent guide books, including "All About Alabama Wildflowers" by Sweet Water Press and "Southeastern Wildflowers" by Crane Hill Press. Today, Jan and Dean keep their wildflower and native plant nursery/shop open to the public by appointment. It is one of the few places gardeners can buy wildflowers grown from Alabama seed sources. For information, call 205-669-4097, or e-mail Jan at jwildflwr@aol.com.

North Alabama Public Gardens

Anniston Museum of Natural History

Anniston Museum of Natural History

800 Museum Drive, Legarde Park
Anniston, AL 36201

One of the Southeast's outstanding natural-history museums extends its collections to the outdoors with several interesting gardens. The Anniston Museum of Natural History's Courtyard Garden creates the ideal microclimate for the cultivation of tropical plants, including cannas, ferns, cycads, gingers, bananas and the largest outdoor collection of palms in Alabama. Nearby, the Wildflower Meadow & Native Garden tells the story of the area's ecology while providing food and shelter for wildlife. Both gardens include attractive water features and quiet seating areas. They are worth visiting regularly, as the gardens are constantly growing in plant diversity and character, thanks to the attention of Dan Spaulding, the museum's botanist and curator of collections, and of local gardener/extension agent Hayes Jackson. Garden hours are dusk to dawn (or sunup to sundown). There is no admission charge to view the gardens. The Courtyard and Wildlife Gardens are handicap accessible. Admission is charged for the museum. Hours of operation are Tuesdays through Saturdays, from 10 a.m. to 5 p.m., and Sundays from 1 p.m. to 5 p.m. (open on Mondays from June through August). For information, call (256) 237-6766 or check out the museum's Web site at www.annistonmuseum.org.

Burritt Museum and Park

3101 Burritt Drive
Huntsville, AL 35801

Sitting on 167 acres atop Monte Sano ("Mountain of Health"), the Burritt Museum and Park offer a splendid view of Huntsville, as well as nature trails, well-tended flower beds and borders around the museum and pioneer kitchen gardens in the living history park. The Accessible Nature Trail is a model for other parks. (The Nature Trails guide booklet is excellent.) With its shade trees, attendant gardens and grand lawn, Burritt is a welcome

Burritt Museum and Park

retreat from the hustle and bustle of the city below (as it has been for centuries.) The grounds are open daily, April through September, from 7 a.m. to 7 p.m., and October through March, from 7 a.m. to 5 p.m. You can visit the grounds for free, but admission is charged to the museum and historic park, which are open from March through mid-December. For museum/historic park hours and information, phone (256) 536-2882 or check out the Web site at www.ci.huntsville.al.us/Burritt/.

CalMac Nursery

160 Ryan Road
Cullman, AL 35057-2754
One of the best places to study herbs –for culinary, ornamental and medicinal purposes – in the Deep South is CalMac Nursery in Cullman. Owners Calera and Ronnie McHenry have been growing these fascinating and useful plants for more than 26 years. Since the opening of their display nursery and garden shop, CalMac has become a mecca for herb gardeners in four states. Located in a pastoral setting near Interstate 65, the nursery offers herb gardeners excellent ideas for growing herbs and decorating with them in the landscape. CalMac is open to the public March 1 through May 31, Tuesdays through Saturdays, from 9 a.m. to 4 p.m. It is open year-round by appointment (even before or after hours and on weekends.) So don't hesitate to call if you are looking for a special herb or plant. (You might luck out and get in on one of the impromptu workshops that Calera hosts.) For information, call (256) 739-3100.

Constitution Village

Constitution Village

109 Gates Ave.
Huntsville, AL 35801
Huntsville's downtown, living-history museum, Constitution Village, offers an entertaining way to learn about old-time kitchen gardening, including herbal "headache bags" pioneer women tucked inside their bonnets. In the summer, the village's small vegetable patch teaches children the story of the "three sisters," corn, bean and squash, the Native Americans' primary food crops. In September, you can sneak a muscadine grape from the old-time arbor. Constitution Village is open Tuesdays through Saturdays, from 9 a.m. to 5 p.m. Admission is $7 for adults, $6 for seniors and youth, and $3 for children 3 and under. For information, call 256-564-8100 or check out the Web site at www.earlyworks.com. NOTE: While in Huntsville, consider taking a walking tour of two nearby historic districts: Twickenham, which contains more than 65 antebellum

Historic Huntsville Walking Tour

structures, and Old Town, which features ornate Victorian homes. Many of these private residences possess charming gardens. For information about the Historic Huntsville Walking Tour, call (256)-533-5723.

Cullman Native Plant Society Wildflower Garden

Sportsman Lake Park
Cullman, AL 35055
Native plant enthusiasts will delight in this four-acre garden set aside by the Cullman County Park and Recreation Board. Well-marked walkways lead through many North Alabama habitats: a meadow, woodland, bog, fern glade and stream bank. (Birmingham landscape architect Jane Reed Ross donated a plan for the trails and the garden entrance.) In late February and early March, spring wildflowers (phlox, trillium, foam flower, spiderwort, fire pink, etc.) emerge from the forest floor. In April, the ferns begin to unfold, and in May, sunny meadow species, such as Black-eyed Susan, take center stage. Located just off U.S. Highway 31 in Cullman, the park is open year-round, sunup to sunset. Admission is free. For information, phone (256) 734-4281.

Huntsville-Madison County Botanical Garden

4747 Bob Wallace Avenue
Huntsville, AL 35805
Organized in 1981, the Huntsville-Madison County Botanical Garden is a gem for garden travelers and locals alike. The showpiece of this 112-acre facility is the Central Corridor Garden, designed by Environmental Planning and Design of Pittsburgh, Pa. The garden is reminiscent of a grand English estate with its formal entryway, circular fountain, long lawn,

lengthy flower borders and soft edges of natural forest. At the far end, the formal Aquatic Garden provides a dramatic climax to this scene. Throughout the garden, paths lead to interesting niches dedicated to wildflowers, perennials, ferns, daylilies, roses, herbs and vegetables. The Tessman Butterfly House offers a treat for children, along with the Garden Railroad and the Vegetable Garden, complete with scarecrows. The Huntsville gar-

Huntsville-Madison County Botanical Garden

den is open November through March, Mondays through Saturdays, 9 a.m. to 5 p.m., and Sundays, from 1 p.m. to 5 p.m.; and April through October, Mondays through Saturdays, 9 a.m. to 6:30 p.m., and Sundays, from 1 p.m. to 6:30 p.m. Admission is free to members. For the general public, the cost is $6 for adults, $5 for seniors and military members, $3 for children 3-18, and free for children 2 and under. For information, phone (256) 830-4447 or check out the Web site at www.hsvbg.org.

Ivy Green

300 W. North Common Street
Tuscumbia, AL 35674
The famous water pump, where a world opened up to a child denied her senses of sight and sound, is one of the most popular sites on

the grounds of Ivy Green, which sits on a 640-acre tract in historic Tuscumbia. The childhood home of Alabama's own Helen Keller, this modest cottage (built in 1820) is surrounded by plants typical of Southern homes: magnolia, mimosa, crepe myrtle, iris and roses. The English boxwoods are as historic as the home, dating back 150 years. The abundant ivy, which gave the home its name, still climbs the cottage walls. The grounds, including the "Clearing," herb gardens and flower beds, are tended by the Helen Keller Garden Club. Ivy Green includes a museum decorated with original furniture and Miss Keller's mementos, including her Braille books and typewriter. It is open Mondays through Saturdays, from 8:30 a.m. to 4 p.m., and Sundays from 1 p.m. to 4 p.m. Admission for adults is $6, for students $2, and for seniors $4. For information, call 205-383-4066 or check out this Web site at www.helenkellerbirthplace.org.

Jackson County Park
2302 County Park Rd.
Scottsboro, AL 35768
This 90-acre county park rests in an unusually pretty setting along the backwaters of the Tennessee River. A few years ago, Vernon Bush, a retired engineer from Huntsville and frequent visitor to the adjacent RV park, got the urge to do some gardening here. Today, the area features an attractive water garden near the restaurant, a lily garden, a colorful central flower bed, several wildflower meadows and an inspiring woodland walk. Along the walking trails, there are hundreds of native azaleas (peaking in April), rhododendrons, mountain laurel and other native shrubs added to enhance the natural beauty. Spring wildflowers and other shade-loving plants (natives and

exotics), ferns, hellebores and naturalizing bulbs have been planted for seasonal interest. Benches and swings along the trails make this garden a welcome retreat. The park itself – with its playground, handicapped accessible fishing pier, swimming and boating facilities and musical stage – serves as a recreational center. It is open year-round from sunup to sundown. For information, call (256) 574-4719.

Noccalula Falls Park & Campground
1500 Noccalula Road (off U.S. Highway 211)
Gadsden, AL 35999
In April, more than 25,000 azaleas turn this park, gardens and campground into a pink and white fairyland. Named after a legendary Indian princess, Noccalula, the park has become a favorite stopover for families and tourists. Appalachian woodlands surround the central feature, a 90-foot waterfall, which drains into the Coosa River. Inside a Pioneer Village, more extensive gardens feature a variety of Southern favorites, such as camellias blooming in winter, roses in late spring, cannas and ginger lilies in summer, plus a water garden and butterfly border. For a contemplative experience, visitors can observe native plants

Noccalula Falls

Etowah County War Memorial, adjacent to Noccalula Falls

on the nature trails near the falls or visit the nearby Etowah County War Memorial, a tribute to the 457 Etowah Countians who lost their lives in Korea, Vietnam and Lebanon. Noccalula Falls is open year-round. Admission is $2 for adults, and $1 for children 6-11 years. For information, phone (256) 549-4663 or check out the Web site at www.gadsden.com/Main_Attractions/Noccalula _Falls/noccalula_falls.html.

Pond Spring, the Wheeler Plantation

12280 State Highway 20
Hillsboro, AL 35643
Step back into the turn-of-the-century pleasure garden of Miss Annie Wheeler at her father's historic plantation near Courtland in Lawrence County. The daughter of a famed Confederate general and Alabama congressman, Joseph Wheeler, "Miss Annie" had an Edwardian fascination with boxwood and a gift for propagating it. A member of the Garden Club of America, she visited gardens all over the country to draw inspiration for Pond Spring. More than 1,000 boxwood, stone pathways, rustic cedar arbors, birdbaths and benches are remnants of a once magnificent garden, that attracted visitors from all over northeast Alabama, according to landscape

architect Carol Blair Lambdin, who is leading the garden restoration. The entire landscape, which includes an 1820 dog-trot house, an 1830 Federal style house, the 1870 Victorian Wheeler house, seven out-buildings and three cemeteries, is worth exploring. Wheeler Plantation is open Thursdays through Saturdays, from 9 a.m. to 4 p.m., and Sundays, from 1 p.m. to 5 p.m. For information, call (256) 637-8513 or visit the Web site at www.wheelerplantation.org.

Pope's Tavern Museum

203 Hermitage Drive
Florence, AL 35630
Little has changed at Pope's Tavern since Andrew Jackson stopped in for a cool drink on his way to New Orleans to battle the British in 1814. Travelers emerging from the wilderness of the Natchez Trace would have been happy to see the watering hole. Today, a restored circular herb garden features culinary historical plants such as sage, thyme, parsley and rosemary, as well as medicinals once used to treat ailing travelers, such as Echinacea, orris root, horehound and feverfew. The garden also includes patriotic bee balm, used as tea during the Revolutionary War as a substitute for English tea. The grounds are dominated by an enormous magnolia and surrounded by maples for fall color. Pope's Tavern is open Tuesday through Saturdays from 10 a.m. to 4 p.m. Admission is $2 for adults and 50 cents for children. For information, phone 256 760-6439 or check out this Web site at www.ci.florence.al.us.

Bibliography

Brookes, John. *The Country Garden.* New York, New York. Crown Publishers, Inc. 1987.

Chaplin, Lois Trigg. *Southern Gardener's Book of Lists.* Dallas, Texas. Taylor Publishing Company. 1994.

Clark, Timothy. *Margery Fish's Country Gardening.* London, England. David & Charles. 1989.

Griswold, Mac. *Pleasures of the Garden: Images from The Metropolitan Museum of Art.* New York, New York. Harry N. Abrams, Inc. 1987.

Griswold, Mac. *Washington's Gardens at Mount Vernon.* New York, New York. Houghton Mifflin Company. 1999.

Martin, Laura C. *Laura C. Martin's Southern Gardens.* New York, New York. Abbeville Press. 1993.

Hobhouse, Penelope and Patrick Taylor. *The Gardens of Europe.* New York, New York. Random House.1990.

Lawrence, Elizabeth. *A Southern Garden.* Chapel Hill, North Carolina. University of Chapel Hill Press. 1991.

Pollan, Michael. *Second Nature.* New York, New York. Dell Publishing. 1991.

Perenyi, Eleanor. *Green Thoughts.* New York, New York Vintage Books. 1981.

Roberts, Edith A. and Elsa Rehmann. *American Plants for American Gardens.* Athens, Georgia. University of Georgia Press. 1996 reprint of 1929 book.

Schinz, Marina. *Visions of Paradise: Themes and Variations on the Garden.* New York, New York. Stewart, Tabori & Chang, Inc. 1985.

Tankard, Judith B. and Michael R, Van Valkenburgh. *Gertrude Jekyll: A Vision of Garden and Wood.* New York, New York. Harry N. Abrams, Inc./Sagapress, Inc. 1989.

Verey, Rosemary. *Rosemary Verey's English Country Gardens.* New York, New York. Henry Holt and Company. 1996.

Very, Rosemary. *The Art of Planting.* Boston, Massachusetts. Little, Brown and Company. 1990.

Welch, William C. and Greg Grant. *The Southern Heirloom Garden.* Dallas, Texas. Taylor Publishing Company. 1995.

Whiteside, Katherine. *Antique Flowers.* New York, New York. Villard Books. 1989.

Wharton, Edith. *Italian Villas and Their Gardens.* New York, New York. Da Capo Press, Inc. 1988 reprint of 1904 book.

Albertville Scarecrow. Photograph by Charlotte Hagood.

This book is dedicated to Ed Givhan.
P.G., J.G., and C.H.